ADVANCE PRAISE

Within the pages of Dr. Anna Kohen's memoir, *Flower of Vlora*, resides real-life drama. The book is a personal account of her family's escape from the Holocaust during World War II (due to the generosity of the Albanian people), as well as Anna's struggles as a child growing up under the communist dictatorship her family endured after the war. Communicated with honesty and courage, *Flower of Vlora* tells the story of Anna's family and of her own well-lived life, when all of it could have gone so very wrong many times. It's the story of a brave and remarkable woman, her incredible passage from war-torn, poverty stricken, and deprived Albania, to the rich and opportunity-filled West – steadily guided by her own goals and by her Jewish family's values. This is an inspirational narrative with many layers, a true tale of a modern-day *Scheherazade* that unfolds over three continents and spans more than 80 years. It's a Balkan story of survival, an American tale of success, and a story of international Jewry. More than anything, *Flower of Vlora* is a life lesson on the merits of living according to your principles, of generously giving back when you can, and of truly caring and loving unconditionally.

Zanet Battinou, Director, The Jewish Museum of Greece

Anna Kohen's detailed and interesting memoir, *Flower of Vlora*, offers readers a look into the full and complex life of a Jewish person of Greek origin whose family miraculously survived the Holocaust. Only 15 percent of Greek Jewry survived, as most lived in Thessaloniki and from there they were all deported to Eastern European camps, where they were murdered. Anna's family fortunately moved from Greece to Albania before the war and there, when the country was taken over by Nazi sympathizers, were hidden in mountain villages among Muslim Albanians. Before the war, the Muslims had been customers of Anna's father, who traveled by donkey village to village selling fabrics. The family belonged to a small ethnic Jewish group, the *Romaniotes*, considered the oldest Jewish diaspora group with its own history and traditions. Because so few Greek Jews survived, there aren't many memoirs about them. *Flower of Vlora* sheds light on one family's fate during the war. Family life and customs are well described, as well as the difficulty of living under communism in Albania after World War II. The author talks about her desire to be well educated and how, despite many challenges, she eventually became a well-known dentist. The story of the family's difficult escape from Albania, after many efforts by the father, first to Greece where the few surviving family members lived, and eventually to the United States, is compelling. Life under communism was very difficult, especially for Jews and for those who would not join the Party, and leaving was very difficult. In the United States the family thrived, and the author became an important spokesperson for her communities. One gets to know Dr. Kohen and her life well – the successes she achieved, and the challenges presented by her husband's health as well as her own. It is truly a unique story of survival against many odds, as well as the triumph of many successes. *Flower of Vlora* is a full and detailed memoir of the life of one very intelligent and ambitious lady.

Michlean Lowry Amir, Volunteer, Holocaust Survivors and Victims Resource Center, United States Holocaust Memorial Museum

In her memoir, *Flower of Vlora,* Dr. Anna Kohen offers the reader the astonishing story of a Greek-Romaniote Jewish family who escaped Ioannina, Greece, moving to Vlora, Albania, right in the nick of time and avoiding the tragic extinction of that ancient community in the Holocaust. It was a Muslim Albanian family in a poor village in the mountains outside Vlora – a family yet to be recognized for their good deeds at Yad Vashem – who saved the Kohens during the height of German occupation in 1944. Later, as little Anna was born and grew up in communist Albania, she courageously embraced in full her Jewish roots, together with the ancient and proud local tradition. Gaining the right to leave Albania as a stateless family during the Cold War was almost an impossible proposition, yet the Kohens managed to do it, unified and fully intact as a family. Anna's brief return to Greece – and then her new and successful professional and personal life in the US – are fascinating examples of hard work, incredible resolve, and strong character. The author is a true role model for young women of any race, creed, or conviction both in her native, beautiful town of Vlora and across the world. *Flower of Vlora* is the story of an incredible life journey, offered through a rich, vivid, and versatile narrative style.

Agron Alibali, Senior Fellow, University of Massachusetts Boston, McCormack Graduate School of Policy and Global Studies, Manchester-by-the-Sea, Massachusetts

I read with pleasure Dr. Anna Kohen's *Flower of Vlora*, an extremely interesting account of her journey through life. The book deals with her personal experiences growing up Jewish in communist Albania, and the life of her Jewish family, who were saved from the Holocaust by the Albanian people during World War II. Later, the book details her studies and accomplishments in Greece and the United States after the family was able to leave the Albanian dictatorship behind.

Flower of Vlora is a tale of Anna's struggle to rise from poverty and lack of freedom to great personal accomplishment and success, which she achieves through the power of her determination, hard work, and relentless ambition. After attaining her educational and professional goals, Anna writes about how she began giving back and assisting others in her community. *Flower of Vlora* will help readers understand how a young woman from a poor country – armed only with courage, wisdom, and the love of her family – was able to break through the glass ceiling in her profession in a new country, and in a totally new language. *Flower of Vlora* is an inspirational text filled with practical advice for working and living with passion and purpose.

Felicita Jakoel, President, Israeli Albanian Friendship Society

———

Dr. Anna Kohen's memoir, *Flower of Vlora*, tells the story of her family's miraculous escape from both the Holocaust and communist Albania. She became a renowned dentist and a prominent intellectual in the US, and (as she writes in her wonderful book) has contributed to the Albanian people and the protection of their human rights wherever they live. She especially worked to aid Albanian refugees from Kosovo during the 1990s war. As a president of AAWO – Motrat Qiriazi in New York, she provided much-needed support to female Albanian immigrants and refugees. She regularly engaged with the Albanian-Israeli Friendship Association in Tirana, meeting with the Albanian minister of culture so we could have a small place for a Jewish museum in Tirana's National Museum. Recounting her family's experience of the salvation of the Jews in her book, Anna brings a unique and important story to the reading public. As she tells us in *Flower of Vlora*, the Albanians who saved the Jews had no religious, political, economic, or cultural biases. Her book is a vivid recollection of this special story, and many other parts of her Jewish Albanian life. Anna honors her Jewish, Albanian, and American roots all through her book, never forgetting her unique

Albanian experience, and writing about it with culture, education, goodness, and brilliance. Most importantly, *Flower of Vlora* is the story of people working together to try and make the world a better place.

Dr. Petrit Zorba, Director of the Albanian-Israel Friendship Association

---

From the first page of *Flower of Vlora,* author Dr. Anna Kohen sweeps the reader into a community of Romaniote Jews living in the repressive, communist country of Albania, who managed to maintain their native Greek language, foods, and Jewish observances despite the government prohibition against all religion. The Kohen family members exemplify resourcefulness, adaptation, and resilience as they manage to thrive in the harshest conditions, emigrate to the United States, and succeed in every endeavor. The book is fast-paced and showcases a truly remarkable family.

Barbara Gilford, Author, *Heart Songs: A Holocaust Memoir*

I read Dr. Anna Kohen's memoir, *Flower of Vlora,* with rare pleasure. I laughed out loud at times as I read her stories from her childhood in Albania, and I felt pain and sadness for how her family was treated by the communist dictatorship. Her book made me feel such a great range of emotions. *Flower of Vlora* is a book written with extraordinary sincerity. I recommend this excellent book to anyone who wants to know the story of how the Albanian people saved the Jews during the Holocaust.

Dr. Shaban Sinani, Author, *Albanians and Jews: The Protection and Salvation*

FLOWER OF VLORA

GROWING UP JEWISH IN COMMUNIST ALBANIA

ANNA KOHEN

a‖p

ISBN 9789493276260 (ebook)

ISBN 9789493276246 (paperback)

ISBN 9789493276253 (hardcover)

Publisher: Amsterdam Publishers, The Netherlands

info@amsterdampublishers.com

Flower of Vlora is part of the series Holocaust Survivor True Stories WWII

Cover design and illustration by Viktor Koen

CONTENTS

PREFACE

After I was finally able to immigrate to the United States in 1970, I realized I had made a remarkable and special journey. That journey had begun many years before in my native Albania, which I managed to leave for Greece in 1966, four years before I made my way to New York. The odds had always been stacked against me and my family because our stateless status as Greek Romaniote Jews trapped us within Albania's repressive and brutal communist dictatorship. I experienced firsthand all the difficulties of my family's years-long effort to acquire proper identity documents and official permission to leave, all while being shadowed by the Albanian secret police. I knew I would like to write our story one day, to share it with my grandchildren, but life has its way of keeping us busy. Between my thriving dental practice, teaching at NYU, and raising my children, I was so busy through most of my life that I just did not have time to write anything, let alone a book.

Then in 1991, the Albanian American newspaper, *Illyria,* began circulating in New York and came to my attention. I placed an ad in it for my dental services, letting the Albanian community know that I spoke the language. I suddenly started to get phone calls at the office from Albanian immigrants and other members of the Albanian community in New York. They would leave messages regarding absolutely everything except needing dental work. They would say, "Dr. Anna, can you find me a job?" or "Dr. Anna, I can do anything. Please help me find work." They wanted me to help them with their careers, their documents, finding apartments, finding babysitters, and so many things that are necessities to newcomers to the city.

I had been an immigrant myself, so I felt a duty to these people. I helped however I could and never said no to anyone. I began to build a strong connection with the Albanian American community. This bond deepened as I helped my own family of 37 Albanian Jews settle in Brooklyn. I led the Albanian American Women's Organization (AAWO – Motrat Quiriazi) for 25 years as its president, and assisted refugees during the Kosovo War. Albanian media and other European media often interviewed me about my nonprofit work. My name does not sound Albanian, so invariably they would ask me why I was so interested in helping Albanians. This would lead me to explain that I was part of a small community of Jews from Vlora, Albania, that I had been born and raised in Albania, and even though I had never held Albanian citizenship, I considered myself an Albanian Jew.

My story surprised the reporters interviewing me. They wanted to know more about how I had been able to escape the country during the communist dictatorship, and whether I was truly Albanian, Greek, Jewish, or something else. They were also curious about the Albanian Jews, of which they knew nothing. After being asked these sorts of questions repeatedly, it dawned on me that my story should one day be written in full, to tell the whole tale, and that it should reach an audience beyond just my grandchildren. The public should know how the Albanian people saved all the local Jews and other Jewish refugees sheltering in the country during World War II.

In so many ways, I have come full circle. I began my life in Vlora, a small, coastal city on a breathtakingly beautiful bay. I am now retired and living in Sarasota, Florida, on a bay that is as gorgeous as the one of my youth. Though my nonprofit work continues, over the past two years I have finally found the time to sit with the old stories of my family – and of the Jewish community that I grew up in during a very dark time in Albania's history – and write this book. I want my grandchildren to know about my own grandmother, Anetta, the very determined and disciplined Jewish woman who raised me to be the successful person I became.

In this book, I reveal for the first time something that most of my Albanian friends likely do not know: that I am not and never have been an Albanian citizen. Despite being born in the country, as a Jew and part of a Jewish family with Greek roots, citizenship was not an option for me. This caused me to have such an unusual and different life from my Albanian peers. I was kept separate from my classmates by the dictatorship, denied access to publicly funded higher education, and had to pay my own way entirely as I pursued my dental studies. My statelessness made me feel different and excluded from the regular Albanian students. Nevertheless, the Albanian Jewish community, small as it was, always found ways to surround me and support me.

My nonprofit work continued and deepened through the years. My efforts have been acknowledged and honored by multiple Albanian presidents and I was even invited to speak at the United Nations. Yet the questions continued to follow me: Who is this Anna Kohen? Why does she want to help the Albanian people?

In November 2019, I was honored by the Jewish Federation of Sarasota-Manatee, where I live now. Soon after I helped organize an amazing event with the Albanian ambassador and other dignitaries at a synagogue in Maryland, just outside of Washington, D.C., that highlighted how the Kosovar Albanians also saved Jews during the war. Two days later, at City Hall in New York City, I was an invited speaker at the celebration of Albania's independence and served as the representative of Albania itself during the event. This made me so proud because Albania's independence had been declared in my city, Vlora, of which I was an honorary citizen.

This whirlwind of events put a new energy into me to write this book. I started work on it in December of 2019, after returning home from that month of ceremonies and celebrations and have toiled at it ever since. It has been so important to me to stay focused and finish it, despite my husband's serious health issues and the isolation of the pandemic. In these pages, I have covered the years 1938 through to the present: telling a lively, funny, and sometimes tense account of my life as the child of Romaniote Jewish immigrants to Vlora, Albania. Arriving in the ancient and picturesque city just before the outbreak of World War II, my parents and grandparents joined a small but established Greek-speaking, Romaniote Jewish community of merchants. My family sold fabrics and also had a dye works. My father traveled by donkey through the Muslim villages located in the mountains all around Vlora. His funny stories are recorded here as they were an important part of my childhood and describe the landscape of Albania and its people. During World War II, those same Muslim families hid my family from the Holocaust – they gave them Muslim names and helped them pretend to be Muslim. Our family members who remained in Greece, including all of my mother's family, were murdered in Nazi death camps.

Flower of Vlora also focuses on the traditions of my family, which we had to celebrate in secret because of the Albanian dictatorship's repressive laws against the practice of religion. Life in Albania was grim under Enver Hoxha, with no possibility of escape. Still, my family and the Jewish community we lived among managed a measure of happiness through togetherness and hard work. Even as a child, I had to work long hours in the family business, always aware of my unique Jewish identity in a country that had so few Jews. I focused on my schoolwork, enjoyed friendships with Muslim and Christian classmates, and wandered the beautiful alleys and markets of my town.

Rendered stateless in a poverty-stricken and repressed country – with no proper documents from Greece and due to our refusal to join the Communist Party (even though that would have allowed us to become Albanian citizens) – my father devised a bold scheme to help us leave Albania for the West. This took years of careful planning, with our family always under the eye of the regime's secret police, the *Sigurimi i Shtetit*. Eventually, we managed to escape the country. I became a dentist first in Greece and then in New York City, learning the craft of dental implants from their inventor, and establishing my own thriving practice.

In this book, you will learn the story of the Albanian Jews and what their lives were like under the communist dictatorship. You will learn more specifically about the lives of my parents and grandparents, and how we kept our religion and Jewish identity alive in a poor country where all religious practice was forbidden. I will share the story of our long-awaited exodus from Albania, and my own story that includes going on to help others leave the country to start new lives in the United States and Israel.

In 2012, I was invited by the Albanian government to visit Tirana and celebrate the centennial anniversary of Albanian independence. My husband, Markus, and I attended dinners with ambassadors and other luminaries. But I had a special mission to accomplish outside of the galas and banquets: I had made up my mind to go to the village where my parents and grandparents were hidden during the war. An Albanian friend hired a driver for us, and Markus and I were taken up to the remote mountain area where my family spent many months pretending to be Muslims to escape the Nazis, going so far as to take on Muslim names.

Some of the elder townsfolk directed us to the family that had saved my parents and grandparents. Unfortunately, the elders from that family and their personal accounts of those days had long since passed, but their children took us to the house where my parents had hidden. We were shown the very room where my parents had spent those months during that terrible time.

Little in my life has been so emotional and moving as when I met the children of the saviors of my family, and their families and loved ones. For years afterward, I tried to get this beautiful Albanian Muslim family acknowledged and honored by Yad Vashem (the World Holocaust Remembrance Center) in Israel, but the officials there ruled that there was not enough qualifying documentation or evidence. In relaying this disappointing news to the family in Albania, in their ever-gracious way, they replied that their parents were not looking for recognition when they hid my parents – they simply did it because it was the right thing to do. They said to me, "Anna, it doesn't matter as long as we stay friends."

In writing this book, I hope to honor that Muslim family as much as my own, to record the stories of my Jewish family in Albania, and to tell the story of the hard work I have done ever since. As I mentioned before, I first intended this book to be just for my grandchildren. But as I have examined the events of my life, I know that this story will hold interest for anyone who might read it. It is a difficult task to share your life story with others, but if it inspires people and gives them hope and encouragement, then it is a great accomplishment. The stories within this book are important and true. I know this because they happened to me. Writing *Flower of Vlora* has been a challenge, a journey, and a labor of love.

It is up to us to live up to the legacy that was left for us, and to leave a legacy that is worthy of our children and of future generations. – Christine Gregoire

INTRODUCTION

In her memoir, *Flower of Vlora*, Dr. Anna Kohen tells her story of being a Romaniote Jew in communist Albania, and how her parents and grandparents survived the Holocaust through the generosity and help of the Albanian people. By way of introduction to her book, my purpose here is to offer a history of Jews in Albania, especially during World War II, and explain just how they were so successfully protected, which is a unique story of tolerance and salvation.

The first wave of Jews to reach Albania followed the Roman destruction of the Jewish Revolt in Judea in 66–73 CE. Secondary waves of Sephardic Jews arrived later, during the Spanish Inquisition in 1492 and the Portuguese Inquisition in 1536. Before World War II, Jews resided in small communities in Albanian towns including Vlora, Berat, Tirana, Elbasan, Korça, Durrës, Shkodra, and Saranda. They freely practiced their religion, had good relations with their neighbors, and enjoyed acceptance among the Albanian people, which was unusual for Europe.

The story of Jews in Albania – and their total salvation by the Albanian people during World War II – is an example of how a country came together to survive the war without giving up their neighbors, as happened in so many other European countries. Let me be clear: not a single Jew in Albania was murdered by the Nazis.

Albania saving its Jews is worthy of singular praise and has left a lasting and positive legacy for the small country in its international relations. The story radiates an important lesson about each of our responsibility toward humanity, the roots of which are outlined as follows:

1. The Albanian *Besa* or "Golden Rule" and the Albanian Mixture of Faiths

For much of the past century, it has been generally accepted that the Albanian people are 70 percent Muslim, 20 percent Eastern Orthodox, and 10 percent Roman Catholic. But that religious breakdown has always been hard to verify, and today is entirely outdated and incorrect. Contemporary Albanians do not care for such distinctions because they see religious beliefs as deeply personal, and the united Albanian nation as rising above what makes its individual people different. The Paragon Encyclopedia of World Facts, published in 2002, reported that 75 percent of the Albanian population is not religious, and these numbers were confirmed by the 2012 Albanian census. Harmony between believers and nonbelievers is a sacred Albanian value and one of the nation's pillars.

Among Albanians, Islam does not have any ethnic base. Albanian Muslims are descendants of Albanian Christians who converted or were forced to convert during the centuries-long occupation by the Ottoman Empire. Ottoman swords cut off heads and took boys away from their families for Janissary service. The stolen Albanian youth were not educated in love, hospitality, harmony, tolerance, or Albanian Besa. They were taught only brutality. The Ottoman Empire and its Eastern Orthodox collaborators cruelly suppressed Albanian culture and education, including outlawing Albanian schools. The 5th through the 15th centuries encapsulated the greater European Dark Ages, but for Albanians what followed in the 15th through the 20th centuries, under the Ottoman Empire, was a second Dark Age.

During the long Ottoman occupation, Albanian uprisings were led by Albanian patriots with Muslim names. From a religious point of view, most Muslim Albanians followed the very liberal *Bektashi* stream of Islam. In the 19th century, leaders of the Albanian Renaissance came from diverse parts of the country and every different religion in the nation. They knew that Albania's religion was actually Albanianism *(Shqiptaria)*. Using this and Besa, they united and enlightened the country.

Group conversion to Islam occurred under duress or the lure of fewer taxes. Even that typically took place by name change only and for the survival of the nation in the face of Ottoman invaders and the enmity – even today – from neighbors under intolerant Eastern Orthodox churches' flags. Even after 1990, Albanian immigrants to Greece found it necessary to change from Muslim to Christian names in order to find work and safety. Regardless, Albanians are a spiritually free people, able to migrate and find success in many countries and amid many religions.

The complete rescue of Albania's Jews during the Holocaust, as well as the safekeeping and survival of all captured Italian soldiers, did not originate from religious motives. All Albanians, regardless of religion, acted and cooperated to save their Jewish neighbors – behaving similarly to the 27,000 persons from 51 countries through 2021 who have been recognized as "Righteous Among the Nations" by Yad Vashem, for their heroic deeds in saving Jews during the Holocaust. For Albanians, religion is neither a representative personal platform, nor a unifying communal one. Therefore, explaining the saving of their Jews cannot be tied to any religious motive among the Albanian population, nor can a religious impulse explain what the Albanians did.

Eighty years ago, at the time of the early events in this book, the average Albanian's education level was low, and learning was only offered in the Albanian tongue. It is unlikely that people read or understood Bibles or Korans, as they were printed in non-Albanian letters and words. Hence, it is unlikely that the Albanians acted to save the Jews due to being inspired on a Besa found in the Koran. There is no Besa in the Koran or in the Bible and no reason that there should be. Albanian communal loyalty was sociological rather than religious. Religious identity came from one's kinship and family. Interfaith marriages were not uncommon, and today are universal.

After World War II, education spread to the Albanian population through a communist filter. For half a century, communist propaganda was forced into peoples' minds, including the children of those who risked their lives and rescued the Albanian Jews. The postwar generations grew up drowning in agitprop. After 1990, at the end of the communist period, people were relieved but exhausted. Albanian *Besa* and *Kanun* had bonded together unbreakably to see the nation through its many difficult times.

Besa and Kanun

Besa is a uniquely Albanian word. Foreigners call the nation "Albania" instead of *Shqipëria,* which is what Albanians call it themselves. Albanians call their language *Shqip*, and themselves *Shqiptarë or Arbëreshë.* The Albanian tongue (Shqip) is the oldest in Europe and is at the root of the tree of all Euro-Indian idioms. Besa is a noble principle that originated wholly on Albanian soil. Besa cannot be found in the Koran, for example, because the Koran is not a fundamental part of Kanun, and both Besa and Kanun predate any holy book.

Kanun is an ethnic code and ancient protocol. It has been the foundation of Albanian society for centuries. The Kanun is a collection of Albanian traditional laws and rights that regulate all aspects of conduct within one's family, village, clan, with members of other clans, and with strangers. In the absence of a functional Albanian state, the Kanun acquires that role. The obligation to the country is demanded by Besa, while the decisions made by wise elders are open and accessible to all in the community. Kanun and Besa survived under Ottoman occupation because the Ottomans had no universal bill of rights that would fairly regulate its subjected peoples' relations. Under the Ottomans' millet scheme, peoples were defined into religious communities, headed by spiritual hierarchies, and legally self-ruled within the Ottoman taxation structures. Vassals to the Sultanate, Albanians had to pay *pro rata* taxes and supply soldiers on demand. The Ottoman millet system became another danger to native Albanian nationhood.

The author of the Kanun was Lekë Dukagjini, a 15th-century Albanian knight and Catholic prince who lived before the Ottoman conquest. He fought Ottoman invaders under Gjergj Kastrioti Skënderbeu, an Albanian national hero and major European figure, and continued the fight after Skënderbeu's death in 1468.

Besa has several meanings ranging from faith, unbreakable trust, and treaty, to "word of honor." It means one has made a sacred pledge to keep one's promise to provide welcome and security. It assures stubborn protection of a guest, even to the point of sacrificing one's own life. Besa is a promise to inherently and spiritually not stay indifferent to someone in need or under persecution, and it requires an Albanian to open their door to anyone in sincere need. It's a pledge to live honestly and truthfully and sacrifice oneself for what is right. Above all, Besa is an Albanian legacy that cannot be erased. Albanians often suffered under more powerful invaders; therefore, as a people, they had a fundamental mission to care for and secure their tongue, heritage, traditions, and history. The expectation is that the genuine friends of Albanians will help with this. Any misuse of Albanian Besa is wrong and invalid.

The ancient *Epos of the Albanian Bravehearts* is a set of legendary stories full of instances of Besa. For example, the story of the "Besa of Konstantin" is still preserved and sung by *Arbëreshes* – Italo-Albanians – in southern Italy's Sicily and Calabria. Konstantin kept his promise to his mother to bring back his sister by resurrecting himself from the grave. In southern Italy, the Italo-Albanians write both in Albanian and Italian; there is an Albanian University and so forth, and from a religious viewpoint, they are Christian. However, they have the same Besa and Albanian culture and tongue as all other Albanians. They have always been in the leadership of Albanian national movements and are a true example of Albanian cultural preservation.

The notion of a guest, which overrules the concept of a foreigner, exists in the Kanun. For example, in book 8: chapter 18 of the text, the Kanun reads: "The house of an Albanian belongs to God and the guest ... Every guest must have the food eaten in the house. The guest must give you their weapon to hold as a sign of guardianship since after you have said welcome, he must have no fear and know that you are ready to defend him against any danger." By Kanun, when a person refuses to honor or follow Besa the society, village, or town condemns him. That person must go into exile because he has lost his respect and reputation. If someone cannot protect his guest, then his honor is spoiled, and his integrity and social position become ruined forever.

The shelter given to a friend is also ruled by Besa. When an Albanian gives his oath, Besa is sealed and is eternal. Besa constitutes the foundation of the Kanun. It is a moral code, a norm of social behavior, and an ancient tradition. Besa given to a friend or guest can never end. When Jews migrated to Albania in high numbers after the Spanish and Portuguese Inquisitions, the Kanun was Albania's governing law that thereby welcomed them.

Besa and the Golden Rule

Besa, an Ethic of Reciprocity, is the Albanian version of the Golden Rule, and it is sacred by Kanun. This cultural precept requires Albanians to "treat others the way you would like to be treated." In another comparison with the Golden Rule, Besa follows this edict:

"That which is hateful to you, do not do to your fellow. That is the whole Torah; the rest is the explanation; go and learn." – Talmud, Shabbat 31a, the Great Principle.

Albanians practicing Besa rescued Jews throughout the Holocaust and at other times in the 20th century. They also saved captured soldiers of the Austro-Hungarian Army in 1917 and the Italian Army in 1943. They cared for Greek citizens and wounded soldiers in World War II and following the Greek Civil War. Albania was a warm sanctuary for Albanians expelled by Serbs from Dardania (*Kosovo Polje*) in 1998 and 1999. That Besa is unique to Albania and is not derived from Islam is underscored by Muslim Bosnia, where Jews were not saved during the Holocaust. In Albania, Jews were dispersed and sheltered in organized safe houses by neighbors who knew what they were doing, who cooperated, who did not spy on one another, and who were assisted by Albanian officials.

Honorably

The communist Hoxha regime closed Albania in the decades after World War II and suppressed the story of the rescue of the Jews for nearly half a century. As a result, many Albanian rescuers and rescued Jews died unrecognized and their stories untold. Sadly, Yad Vashem has awarded "Righteous Among the Nations" to only 69 Albanians instead of the hundreds who deserve the honor.

Albania's saving of its Jews came to international attention for the first time when US Congressman Tom Lantos and former Congressman Joseph DioGuardi visited Tirana in June 1990. They received from the Albanian President a thick dossier of letters that rescued Jews had mailed to their Albanian rescuers since 1945. The messages did not reach the Albanian rescuers because the State Security (Sigurimi i Shtetit) censored and hid them within their archives. That pack of letters was afterward sent to Yad Vashem and constituted the basis for the book *Jewish Rescue in Albania* by Harvey Sarner. Since then, the story of the salvation of Albania's Jews has been acknowledged, researched, conferenced, referenced, and published.

Albanian Besa is uniquely and wholly Albanian. It is neither for sale nor on sale. It is inappropriate to use Albanian heritage, the Besa, on any religious platform or for non-Albanian purposes. It is inaccurate to say that any specific Albanian religious community saved the Jews instead of the entire Albanian population. It is also incorrect to view the Albanian people and the good they have done through the lens of any one religious belief.

2. The Rescue of Jews in Kosovo

For Albania, World War II began when the Italian army invaded their country on April 7, 1939. As a result, Albania lost its independence to the Italian Colonial Empire. Albania was occupied by first the

Italians and then the Germans, throughout World War II. As they conquered the Balkans, the Germans eventually gained control of northern Kosovo, including the town of Mitrovica and its valuable mine, Trepça. Without that mine, the German military could not have kept its war machine moving. From April 1941 to November 1944 central and southern Kosovo, western Macedonia, and south and southeastern Montenegro were administratively combined by the Germans with Albania. These were Albanian-inhabited areas that European powers had previously taken away from Albania and given to Yugoslavia. Only Çamëria, a province in Lower Albania that Greece gained control of in March 1913, did not become part of Albania during World War II. The Romans had called this region Epirus, and its capital was Ioannina, which had a vibrant Romaniote Jewish community at the onset of the war, including the author's family.

Albanian archives help to give a view of what happened in Kosovo during World War II. Seeking safety from Nazi persecution, Jews began pouring into central Albania from the Kosovo capital of Pristina. Wartime Albania would not see even a single Jew forced to wear any badge or sign that would distinguish him or her as a Jew, as had happened wherever the Nazis took control, making it a place of safety and refuge.

In neighboring Serbia, antisemitism was well established before World War II, and encouraged by politicians, military officers, and the Serbian Orthodox Church. These conditions allowed it to flourish during the war. On January 20, 1942, a meeting of senior Nazi officials took place in the Berlin suburb of Wannsee. Called the Wannsee Conference, its outcome yielded the decision to complete "the final solution to the Jewish question." In the conference, the number of Jews to be exterminated in each of the European countries was identified. Within three months and without German help, the Serbian state and Chetniks made Belgrade the first *Judenfrei* (free of Jews) city in Europe and liquidated almost every Jew in Serbia. Serbian Jews trying to escape the Holocaust fled to Kosovo with dreadful tales of what was happening.

The Jews of Kosovo numbered 409 persons. The Italian Army

gathered Kosovo's Jews, as well as those caught entering from Serbia and other countries, into its military camp in Pristina (on the site of today's Faculty of Philology of the University of Pristina) – more than 3,000 Jews in total. These detainees were in constant danger from Nazis and Serbs and their only hope of escape was to Albania. Officials knew that sooner or later the Nazis would put them to death; therefore, a plan was devised.

First, the Prefect of Pristina, Hysen Prishtina, and the Secretary of the Pristina Town Hall, Preng Uli, falsely declared that the camp was infected by typhus and needed to be evacuated. Next, Halim Shaqir Spahia transported almost all "infected" Jews by trucks or buses to Albanian towns including Kruma, Kukës, Burrel, Tirana, Durrës, Kavaja, Berat, and Vlora. Also involved in carrying out this lifesaving plan were Arsllan Mustafa Rezniqi, Kol Biba, Hasan Rrem Xerxa, and Dr. Spiro Lito.

Albanian officials in Tirana and Pristina organized this rescue of the Kosovo Jews in cooperation with the highest powers in wartime Albania. The Albanian officials in the Prefecture of Pristina related to that operation, who should be recognized for their humanity and bravery, also included: Riza Drini, Prefect of Pristina 1941–1942; Hysen Prishtina, Prefect of Prishtina 1942–1944; and Preng Uli, Secretary of Prishtina Town Hall, 1941–1944. Even in the wake of these heroic efforts, a few Jews chose not to leave. When the German army reached the Kosovo camp in September 1943, their fates were sealed.

Halim Shaqir Spahia and his brothers were businessmen from the town of Gjakova. They used their office buildings in Kukës, Kruma, Prizren, Tirana, and Durrës to lodge Jews before they found safe houses in Albanian towns and villages or reliable ways to travel by sea from Durrës to safer countries. Arsllan Mustafa Rezniqi built a second home in his garden to house Jewish families. In total his family rescued 42 Jewish families. In 2008, he received the title of "Righteous Among the Nations" from Yad Vashem. Arif Musa Aliçkaj was an employee of the Town Hall of Deçan. Like Preng Uli, he made and issued false passports and documents for Serbian Jews by registering them as Bosnian. With such papers, they were able to travel south to safer locations in Albania. Hasan Rrem Xerxa from

Gjakova transported Jews in his car from Shkup to Deçan and deeper into Albania. Other Albanian families sheltered Jews in Kosovo until they ensured their safe journey to inner Albania. To name just a few of them: the families of Bajram Voca and Sejdi Sylejmani in Mitrovica, the Sabit Haxhikurteshi family in Pristina, the families of Ruzhdi Behluli and Riza Çitaku in Gjilan, the families of Hasan Shala Mullashabani and Asim Luzha in Gjakova, and the Belegu family in Peja.

Through governmental channels, Jews were sent from Pristina to central Albania by the dozens, then hundreds. Since the transfers were made in haste, it is common to find Albanian archived documents written in Italian or Albanian with lists of names and next to each a number (just a numeral) which represents the number of family members transported under that name. Publications by authors such as Harvey Sarner, Martin Gilbert, Ariel Scheib, Gavra Mandil, and others have mentioned those rescues.

An archived dossier (F.152, V. 1942, D. 319) attests to the relocation of 551 Jews from Pristina to Berat in 1942. The document records 87 individuals and 94 heads of families (listed as *con la famiglia*). In a report dated March 30, 1942, the Internal Ministry of Albania ordered the Prefects in the "liberated lands" to reposition all Jews of their districts into "old Albania." Two days later, on April 1, the Internal Ministry of Albania ordered the Prefecture of Prizren to send all Jews to a gathering field in Kosovo. Trucks soon arrived and took them and 69 other Jews from the prison of Pristina to Albanian Kavaja, Burrel, Kruja, and Shijak. On April 5, a group of 100 Jews arrived in Berat, in central Albania. Some days later, 79 Jews from the town of Peja, in Kosovo, came to Preza, near the Albanian capital of Tirana.

Another remarkable story documents 256 Jewish families, totaling 860 persons, who temporarily sheltered in Kosovo before relocating to central Albania in 1942 and 1943. This comprehensive list comes as a courtesy of Dr. Haim Abravanel, of the Kosovo-Israeli Friendship Association. It is a list of 55 Yugoslavian Jews appearing on pages 101–102 of the book *Jevreji Kosova i Metohije*, by P. D. Ivanov (Beograd, 1988), who reported that they were transported from Pristina to the concentration camp of Bergen-Belsen in 1944. But documents in the

Central Archive of Albania prove that they survived the Holocaust by being relocated to central Albania. This information, with extensive archival references, saw publication for the first time in the book *Jews in Albania: The Presence and Salvation,* by Shaban Sinani.

After the Italian Army capitulated on September 8, 1943, the Albania *de jure* reestablished its independence, and on October 16, declared its neutrality. *De facto*, the war atrocities, military operations, and fighting continued without interruption, though the Nazis and their weakening Wehrmacht recognized Albania's independence and neutrality. Things looked better in an instant and 185 Jews from Pristina who were safely residing in Berat went as families back to Pristina. When they arrived there, however, they found themselves trapped. Some managed to return to Berat, while others remained in hiding. Khaim Adizhes was a small boy when his family returned to the city. According to his testimony, when the German Army was making massive arrests, Serbian neighbors reported any known Jews. As a result, many were detained, of the rest, as many as possible escaped to inner Albania. Those arrested were sent to Sajmishte Camp near Belgrade and later to Bergen-Belsen. A few of them survived the war, Khaim Adizhes among them. The arrests and transportation to the Sajmishte Camp occurred in May and June of 1944. Khaim Adizhes and his family were not on the *Transportenliste* of August 1944 from Pristina to Sajmishte.

The salvation of the Jews in Kosovo was not so different from that of those in inner Albania. Those two stories are complementary parts of the overall salvation of Jews by Albanians and as a whole they can be jointly considered and understood. Jews were rescued by the active efforts of Albanian governments and the people in wartime Albania. When the German Army entered Kosovo in September 1943, almost all Jews of Kosovo had by then been relocated to inner Albania. Acknowledgment of this comes from the *Encyclopedia of Jewish Communities,* or *Pinkas HaKehillot Yavan* (Yad Vashem, 1998, pp. 413–425), which states that the Germans requested from the Albanian government in the spring of 1944 a list of Jews and permission to act on them. The Albanian administration did not supply the records and declared that the Jewish community was an internal Albanian affair and gave no consent. Albanians saved Jews wherever they had jurisdiction over them. The Çamëria coastal regions, including Anna Kohen's ancestral Ioannina, was not part of Albania during World War II, and the Jews there were exterminated.

In 2005, the United Nations designated January 27 as International Holocaust Remembrance Day. The Albanian Parliament endorsed this day and called it, "The Day of Remembrance." Albania, a sanctuary for thousands of Jews, officially organizes activities surrounding this date each year.

From the beginning of World War II until its end, millions of European Jews fell under the Nazi regime. They faced arrest, destruction of property, violence, expulsion from homes, family separation, and mass murder both at the point of arrest and in concentration camps. The number of camps and the immensity of the entire operation is utterly staggering. Not all concentration camps became extermination camps, but many did.

After the Night of the Broken Glass on November 9, 1938, the desperate situation compelled Jews to flee wherever they could. Many were unable to protect their children, their families, or themselves. Throughout that time, those of brave and moral conscience tried to help the Jews. In Germany and Austria, foreign diplomats and nongovernmental associations based in Britain were at the center of the salvation efforts. US and British governmental and civic projects started to settle refugee Jews in Britain, the US, and other sympathetic countries.

German and Austrian Jews who had fled to Italy soon began leaving because of laws introduced against them by Mussolini's government two days before the Night of the Broken Glass. On December 30, 1939, on British government demand, Yugoslav authorities stopped a ship on the Danube River with 1,310 Jews on board, bound for British Palestine. The Yugoslavs put those Jews in jail in Shabac. After six months, 207 Jewish children under 16 years of age received immigration certificates for British Palestine. The remaining 1,003 Jews perished when the German Army occupied Yugoslavia in April 1941. The Bulgarian Army gathered Jews in Macedonia and its occupied areas of Greece and transported them to

Poland's extermination camps. The German Army did the same in its zones in Greece. Many never got to the camps because they died on the journey due to confinement, inadequate nutrition, and lack of drinking water.

Despite the atrocities going on all around it, Albania retained its dignity. Albania saved her Jews and every Jew who could reach her borders. The fact simply is that all Jews survived in Albania. They were not spied on or surrendered to the Nazis. They were not prohibited from entering the country because there were no immigration quotas against them. They suffered no abuse, and no one took their possessions. They were not disturbed by any special laws enacted against them. In other words, they found Besa from every Albanian they encountered, every Albanian who opened a door to them, every Albanian official who reviewed their papers, and every Albanian who refused to stand indifferent.

After the Italian Army capitulated in September 1943, 25,000 Italian soldiers also went into hiding and were saved in Albania. It was common for an Albanian family to conceal either Italians or Jews during that time. Regardless of faith, the entire Albanian population responded directly or indirectly as a unified culture by resisting the Holocaust and saving all Jews within its reach. There was not one Jew in Albania who perished due to the Holocaust. Fourteen Jews were killed in battles as members of the anti-fascist Albanian forces or from being caught in the line of fire.

Albania made itself into a lifesaving ark for persecuted Jews. Traces of evidence exist in the towns and villages of Mitrovica, Prishtina, Gjilan, Deçan, Peja, Gjakova, Shkodra, Kruja, Tirana, Berat, Kavaja, Durrës, Elbasan, Librazhd, Korça, Dibra, Burrel, Fier, Lushnje, Vlora, Delvina, Përmet, and Gjinokastra. Jews fled toward Albania and Albanian regions because they knew they would not suffer persecution there. They knew of the absence of immigration quotas, and that no religious or nationalist contempt awaited them, and no genocide, and that Albania was a sanctuary. Jews knew that Albanians had Besa, which meant an open door to anyone in need. They saw that Albanian Jews lived a life like everyone else.

Research by Apostol Kotani, Shaban Sinani, and others shows

that at least 3,280 Jews were saved in Albania by the end of World War II. Yad Vashem has received this list. This number does not include Jews who entered Albania with false passports or names (i.e., with Albanian names on Albanian papers), or those who came illegally (i.e., those sheltered in various villages), or those who might be on lists by other authors, or those not yet recognized by research. The latter is significant because it is common to see archived records having only the family or group leader's name and other accompanying family members as merely an attached number under the heading "together with their families." The compilation of research on rescued Jews continues.

The Lieutenant of the Italian King to wartime Albania, Francesco Jacomoni, in his book, *La Politica dell' Italia in Albania (The Italian Politics in Albania),* asserts secret cooperation for saving Jews between the Albanian Prime Minister, Mustafa Merlika Kruja, and the chief of Confidential Affairs in the Italian Foreign Ministry, Luigi Vidau. One case includes providing Albanian passports with Albanian names to more than 300 Yugoslav Jews who had taken refuge in the Kosovo region. In early April 1942, about three months after the Wannsee Conference, the German Consul General showed detailed information of Jews by name and address to Albanian Prime Minister Kruja and required him to deliver them. Kruja immediately sent his officials to Kosovo to issue Albanian passports to those Jews and then transported them to Gjinokastra in southern Albania by SATA company buses. The reply to the German Consul General several days later was that the information had been incorrect. Another cited case had to do with the secret orders given by Luigi Vidau to Italian Embassies or Consulates to issue Albanian passports with Albanian names to Jews from Germany, Bohemia, Poland, Hungary, and Romania. With such passports, Jews traveled to Albania, to or through other countries, or received entry visas into states accepting immigrants by quotas.

On July 10, 1943, Allies landed in Sicily (they would advance into mainland Italy on September 3). The fascist government of Benito Mussolini was deposed on July 25, and Italian authority over Albania was in rapid decline. In August Albanian Interior Minister

Kol Bib Mirakaj issued more than 2,000 Albanian passports to Jews, enabling them to travel by sea to southern Italy. The documentary film *The Albanian Code* by Professor Yael Katzir brought just such a salvation case to renewed attention. The family of Annie Altaratz-Francis, after escaping from Macedonia to Albania, received accommodation in the Tirana suburbs. Annie Altaratz-Francis was a child when her family fled Albania by boat to Italy in August 1943. The challenge for making the film was that the rescuers and the rescued have all died, taking their stories with them.

In the film, Annie Altaratz and her two daughters (one born in Israel and the other born in the US), thank the children of those rescuers they could find. They meet the child of the Albanian rescuer from Macedonia who guided her family to Albania, and the son of her rescuer in Tirana.

The story of Jews saved by Albanians has become widely acknowledged. In Jerusalem, the Yad Vashem institution has documented and recognized as "Righteous Among Nations" 69 Albanians for their deeds in saving Jews during the Holocaust. The story of Albania's salvation of its Jews spreads from the ongoing work of historians, activists of the Albanian national cause, civic associations, scholars, journalists, politicians, friends, and benevolent persons. Albanians saved Jews without any vested interest or reward other than Besa.

Jews who were rescued in Albania and survived the Holocaust continued their paths either in Albania or other countries. Jews who remained in Albania after the end of World War II left legacies of accomplishment in many fields. They worked hard and lived like all other citizens. Their contributions to Albanian life are well respected.

The communist governing regime in Albania ended in 1991. By that time, everything in the country was in ruin. As a result, one and a half million Albanians, including the rescuers and the remaining Jews, emigrated abroad. Jews left Albania as a group in the spring of 1991 and were a small portion of the waves of hundreds and thousands of Jews who relocated to Israel from Eastern Europe.

The life of an individual is like a flower. The lives of the populace are like a field of flowers. And flowers have roots. Nurture them and be rewarded with the beautiful flowers that result.

Many have asked me: Why did the Albanians save their Jews?

My answer has always been: Why not?

Saimir A. Lolja, author of *The Nation-Free Recipe*, Toronto, June 2021

In honor of my grandmother, Anetta.
In memory of my parents, Nina and David, and my brother, Elio.
To my grandchildren Alex and Dylan, and my sunshine, Alana.
To my dear husband, Markus, for allowing me to dig deep and bring all my fears, hopes, and dreams to the surface, so I could share them from my heart.
And lastly, to everyone who wonders if I am writing about them. I AM!

1

MY ANCIENT CITY

I have such fond memories of my early life in Vlora, Albania – the small, ancient city on the Adriatic coast where I grew up. I was born in Vlora in August 1945, right after the end of World War II. Everything I remember of that time still feels vivid and bright. The irony was that as a child, I didn't know what was really happening. My parents had to eke out a threadbare existence from the time they came out of hiding, after the war, and for them daily life was bitterly hard.

Every Albanian since the end of the war had to live under the brutal authoritarian rule of Enver Hoxha, our feared communist dictator, and his murderous secret police, the *Sigurimi i Shtetit* (State Security). We lacked most necessities and had none of the luxuries of the West. All communication was monitored, foreign travel was prohibited, and escape was totally impossible. There was no longer a middle class, just us poor commoners and the pampered, ruling members of the vile dictatorship. Hoxha had ruined our relationship with our more prosperous neighbor, Yugoslavia. In the late 1950s, in the middle of a terrible drought, the Soviets in Moscow halted grain shipments to us. In the Albania of my youth, famine was always close at hand, but my parents found ways to keep that dark truth from us.

In this way, my siblings and I were able to have wonderful childhoods.

My family and I were Romaniote Jews, a very small and special community of Greek-speaking Jews. Neither Sephardic nor Ashkenazi, Romaniote Jews are much older than either of those celebrated branches of Judaism. Despite being little known, the Romaniote Jews are in fact the oldest of all the Jewish communities who have ever lived in Europe.

Dating back at least 2,300 years to the time of Alexander the Great, the Romaniote Jews established communities in many Greek cities like Ioannina, where my parents and grandparents were from. Through two millennia, the Romaniotes made their livings as artisans, craftsmen, and farmers, and were more typically poor than wealthy. Officially named the *Romaioi* during the Byzantine Empire, we Romaniotes spoke and dressed just like our Greek Christian neighbors, with little to tell us apart from them. Yet we faithfully practiced our Jewish traditions at home and made marital *shidduch* matches within our community.

My family surname, Kohen, is a common Jewish name that means my father's ancestors were priests in the Temple of Jerusalem. Usually spelled "Cohen," ours was spelled with a K in the Greek manner since the letter C does not exist in the Greek alphabet. At home, we spoke not Yiddish, Hebrew, or even Albanian, but almost exclusively Greek, which was my parents' native tongue. We practiced ancient Jewish liturgical traditions dating to the time of the Second Temple, which were unique to the Romaniotes among all other European Jews.

Nearly every Romaniote Jew was exterminated by the Nazis during the Holocaust. My parents and grandparents did not know it at the time, but their move to Albania just before the war saved their lives. By the end of World War II, there were nearly no Jews left alive in Axis-occupied Greece. On March 25, 1944, the nearly 2,000 Romaniote Jews of our native Ioannina, including my mother's entire family, were deported to Auschwitz. Just over two weeks later, on April 11, 1944, the Romaniote Jews of Ioannina were gassed. Today, few Romaniote Jewish synagogues remain in the world. There are roughly half a dozen in Greece, two in Israel, and just one in the Western Hemisphere – the Kehila Kedosha Janina Synagogue and Museum on Manhattan's Lower East Side. That we survived at all is a miracle. A miracle of Albanian generosity.

My father, David, was an accountant, and my mother, Nina, worked at the port of Vlora as an administrative assistant. I had three siblings – my brother Elio, who was two years older than me, and my brother Abe, who was two years younger than me and nicknamed "Mimi," and finally my sister Alice, who was four years younger than me and nicknamed "Aliki." We lived in a rented, two-story, attached house on a narrow cobblestone street in the old city of Vlora. The street's name was Thoma Byko, but everyone called it *Rruga e Çifutëve* in Albanian (which was very derogatory and means "Street of the Jews"), because that was where all the Romaniote Jewish families lived, about ten families in total. We had extended family living on the Street of the Jews, and my father's parents lived with us in our home – my wonderful grandparents, Anetta and Elia.

Unlike Greece, Albania managed to save its Jews during World War II, but despite this, once Hoxha came to power he outlawed all religion. At that time, Vlora was 70 percent Muslim, with smaller populations of Catholics and Greek Orthodox. We Jews were a tiny minority, perhaps one percent. Albania had long been a small, diverse country of Muslims, Christians, Jews, and other ethnic groups living together peacefully – a true European crossroads. Now, we all had to renounce our religions for our own safety, in response to Hoxha's cruel edicts.

No matter what the dictatorship decreed about religion, to me, being Jewish in Vlora was wonderful. My parents and grandparents had immigrated to Albania from Ioannina in 1938 and were rather recent arrivals. Jews of all sorts of backgrounds formed a closely knit community in Vlora. There were other Greek Jews from Ioannina who had arrived much earlier than my parents, and our families were very friendly. I remember going every night to our neighbor Moize Negrin's house and bringing chestnuts to grill. We would eat Greek food and sing Greek songs. I still remember those lively old ballads about love and happiness. My mother used to lead everyone in song and the children had a wonderful time hearing the adults talk about the past and how things used to be in Greece. On "The Street of the Jews," ours was a simple but happy life.

There was a rabbi named Isak Koen who lived in the center of town, though we could not call him "rabbi" because of the restrictions against religion. All the Vlora Jews gathered at his house during the holidays to celebrate, even though this was forbidden. We managed to skirt the repressive religious laws and meet in this clandestine manner for many years, secretly preserving our Jewish faith. But at Passover we celebrated with my Aunt Zhuli – my father's sister – and her family, just our two families. I called my aunt *Thia Zhuli,* thia being the Greek word for aunt. Through our connections in the cloth and fabrics trade, which our family did with the villages around Vlora, we were able to gather the foods we needed for our holiday meals. We cooked Greek cuisine: big salads with feta cheese and olives, stuffed grape leaves and stuffed peppers, and I especially remember *Iman Baialdi*, a Turkish recipe of vegetables and beef that was cooked slowly and was so delicious. We also had a spinach dish, *Llahan*, that was like a pie without the crusty dough. During the holiday, our grandmother would make Llahan with a gold lira coin baked inside, and whoever discovered the coin as they ate was lucky and got to keep it. These were grand but secret celebrations, as everyone else in Albania lived at that time on rations. No one outside our house or the Jewish community knew of our special family events.

It was at one of those Passover celebrations, when I was around 10 or 12, that something happened that set a tenor for my life. During the meal, everyone was drinking Albanian raki: a sweetened, sometimes anise-flavored, alcoholic concoction made from grapes that was similar to Greek ouzo, but stronger. Even young children like me were allowed to have some. I was seated next to my older cousin, Pepo Kohen, who was smoking, and some of his cigarette ashes landed in my small raki glass and I drank them. Soon the dinner was over, and I felt so intensely woozy that I had to go and lay down. Thia Zhuli sat beside me on the bed and listened to me as I talked aloud in my delirium. My eyes were closed and I began to have conversations with relatives I had never met; my Thia Nina David in Greece and my Uncle Isaak Ben Avraam in Israel.

In the dream, I had left Albania and was greeting my aunt and uncle and telling them how very happy I was to meet them. Thia Zhuli stayed with me all through the night because she was so worried about me. The next morning, she told me that I must be a medium because I spoke of things while I was asleep that I could not have known. Some years later when I left Albania and finally met the aunt and uncle I had been "talking" to that night, our conversations progressed much in the same way as they had in my dreams. It seemed as if I had peered into the future all those many years before.

Throughout my life I have had this unusual ability to sense things, especially about people's character and trustworthiness. This sixth sense has helped me to avoid certain difficulties during my working years. I really have felt like a medium, and often remember Thia Zhuli's words to me about my abilities.

In our close and tightly bound family, chief among our leaders was my paternal grandfather, Elia, who lived with us along with his wife, my grandmother Anetta. A well-educated man, he ran a garment-dyeing business. Since my mother worked outside of the home, I was raised primarily by my grandmother, who became a stabilizing force for me and was among the most influential individuals of my life. My grandfather maintained our family discipline. He was very strict, and we obeyed him like soldiers because at times he truly scared us. He insisted that we do things properly and taught us right from wrong. Although he was not considered Orthodox, his education and background gave him the ability – rare in those days – to read the proper books for Passover. He recited the Haggadah step-by-step to perfection and my siblings and I had to follow his lead. Seders were lengthy but read accurately and completely in the ancient Romaniote language of Greek Jews. We all took great pride in this.

Our Romaniote language was the key difference between us Kohens and our Jewish neighbors from other parts of Europe, many of whom spoke Yiddish or even Spanish. Romaniote blends Hebrew and Greek similarly to how Yiddish – the historic language of

Ashkenazi Jews of Central and Eastern Europe – combines Hebrew and German. To this day, I still dream in the language of my roots. Our language helped us communicate privately among family and Romaniote friends. It also helped to protect us. If a *Sigurimi i Shtetit* (secret-police spy) came into the front room of our home where we did business, we would whisper to each other, *Lasare ta diburim* ("watch what you say"). When we suspected someone of coming in to shoplift, we would whisper, *Ta inajim* ("keep your eyes open"). The person we spoke of couldn't understand us or know what we were up to, and there was a sense of power in that.

2

FOOD LINES

Vlora was founded by the seafaring Greeks in the sixth century BC. Because of its location on the Adriatic Sea, it was jealously fought over by the Romans, Goths, Ottomans, Nazis, and Soviets. Today, Vlora is a prosperous resort town with gorgeous beaches, attracting well-heeled tourists from around the world. But the Vlora I knew in the 1950s and 1960s was a hardscrabble place that always felt as if it were covered by dark clouds.

Finding enough food to feed a family under Hoxha's communist rule demanded patience and stamina. Common people had to stand in ration lines that could stretch on and on and take hours to get through. It was a job not well suited to older people, particularly during the winter months when temperatures were freezing or below. The young were obviously far better equipped for waiting outside. In the Kohen household, that unenviable job went to me.

To help myself manage this difficult task, I devised a system of my own making. I would wake up at two o'clock in the morning, get dressed, and hurry to the grocery store where I would put a rock down at the door to mark my place in line. I'd leave and return two hours later. By that time, there might be ten people lined up, gossiping to pass the time as people then always did, and often the rock I had placed would be missing. So, I would announce to the waiting line in a very loud voice, "Who moved my rock that I put here at two o'clock this morning? I want my rock back!"

Somebody would always fess up and return my rock to its place by the door. I developed quite a reputation for myself. Everybody knew me by my nickname, Eni. The adult women in line were afraid of me because they knew I wouldn't hesitate to throw an all-out fit right there on the street if somebody moved my rock or refused to return it. At 6:30 a.m., I'd bring my mother with me and show her the rock I'd left at the door hours earlier that marked her place in line. My little system worked! I'd leave my mother there and hurry back home to get ready for school. She would be the first in line to buy food when the store opened, which allowed her to get that chore done and still arrive to work on time.

Because of my rock system, our family usually had enough meat and bread for our meals despite the endless rationing going on in the country. I made my 2 a.m. visit to the store nearly every night, rain or shine, always placing my rock at the door to secure a place at the head of the line for my mother.

3

THE FAMILY BUSINESS

My grandfather, Elia, left his native Greece in 1938 because of the economic pressure he was feeling in the troubled Greek economy. As his fabrics business in Ioannina failed, an offer to help another Jewish businessman salvage what remained of his own fabrics company after a devastating warehouse flood came along. The opportunity was not too far away in Vlora, Albania, and my grandfather brought his wife, Anetta, and their 16-year-old son, David (my father) with him. After helping to save the other man's business, my grandfather decided to stay in Vlora and start a business of his own.

In a bleak country where nearly every adult woman wore solid black, my grandfather entered the clothes-dyeing trade. One would think that dyeing clothing black would not bring in much income, but my grandfather cast aside all negative thinking; he had to make a living for his family, after all. He set into motion an entrepreneurial gamble that simply should not have worked in a repressive, communist country. But work it did! That was the sort of determination my grandfather had.

While he went about running the family dyeing business, my grandmother Anetta handled the everyday household tasks. Unlike most people in Vlora, particularly the non-Jews, my grandparents had some real education. My grandmother had finished seventh grade, which was very unusual in those days for any girl. After that she also attended the Alliance Française in Ioannina with all the other Jewish girls, which was a way to acquire cultural studies when other educational opportunities were not allowed or available. Because of this, she spoke French quite well. Though I don't know if my grandfather finished high school, through his Hebrew education he became as knowledgeable as a rabbi and was able to teach us the correct Jewish practices and traditions.

Their educations gave my grandparents a significant advantage in Albania, especially when it came to business. Their knowledge and smarts enabled them to see beyond the food lines, the restrictions on travel, the constraints over possessing money, and the other difficult facets of Albanian life. In a hopeless nation choking under the heel of a greedy, ruthless dictator, my grandparents possessed real imagination – something I have come to know is among the rarest of personal assets. Creativity, too, was in short supply in Albania at that time. Most people we knew seemed beaten down and depressed, but our family had creativity and ingenuity in abundance. Since both of my parents worked long hours, my siblings and I were essentially raised by our grandmother. All the traits that she possessed when it came to work and finding solutions to challenges, she passed on to us.

As my grandfather's business grew and he got older, my mother left her job at the port to train under him and learn the dyeing process, including mixing the dyes and working with the fabrics. It wasn't easy work. We were able to buy the dyes we needed from Greece through my Aunt Nina (the one I dreamed of as a child), who still lived there. I don't know exactly how all of that worked and there were always stories about my father needing to travel to Tirana and elsewhere to get the dyes from people he knew. When a customer would come to our house with a gray suit and wanted it dyed black, we made sure to give him a well-dyed black suit. Albanians owned very few good clothes, and they wanted their clothes to look refreshed from time to time. Having their clothes dyed cost less than buying new clothes, so we were always very busy.

This was how my grandfather managed to start and operate one of the only private businesses in Albania during the communist period. We filled a need for the community and for some reason the communists turned a blind eye to what we were doing. I know that my grandfather never paid bribes and was honest in everything he did. The Sigurimi i Shtetit could have shut us down, but they didn't. I think our work helped to keep the community happy, and we were left alone because of that.

Our dyeing business was small but grew steadily. When we added scarf dyeing, our business began to do even better. Scarves were a fashion mainstay of Albanian women. Most women tied scarves over their hair, regardless of the time of year, so this was an important business for us.

At work and at home my father was very outgoing. He had a big circle of friends in Vlora, and he'd tell fortunes for them by reading Turkish coffee grounds in their cups in the traditional way. He had a great sense of humor and knew just what people wanted to hear. If he gave a reading to a single woman, he would predict that she would soon marry. If he gave a reading to someone he knew had money problems, he would say they would soon be receiving a package in the mail. My father loved to make people laugh, and he loved telling stories. One old story I always adored hearing him tell was from when he was young, before the war and the communist period. To help make his living, he got a cart and donkey and traveled to all the Muslim villages in the mountains around Vlora, selling the beautiful fabrics he purchased in Naples.

There wasn't much going on in those farming villages, and because my father was young and handsome, the housewives were always happy to see him. They would run out of their homes as he arrived and pay pretty much any price he asked because they liked how he flirted with them. Usually, all the men would be away at work, and had no idea that their wives at home were swooning over the fabric salesman. But one day, one of the husbands – Osman Bej – came home early with two barrels of fine olive oil. When he saw the wives of the village flirting with my father at his donkey cart laden with colorful fabrics, he set down his oil barrels and began shouting at him, "What are you doing here, cheating our women out of our money!" This caused a big commotion with my father rushing to collect his fabrics and his money, and Osman Bej hollering at him. It only ended when everyone suddenly noticed that my father's donkey was drinking Osman Bej's containers of fine olive oil. Before my father could stop the donkey, the stubborn animal had drunk it all.

Osman Bej demanded immediate payment in gold coins from my father – or else he would take him to court! My father kept his cool. He agreed with Osman Bej and told him, "You are correct! The donkey is at fault. You take him to court, and I will come as a witness."

That was my favorite of my father's stories, and I would go on to tell it to my granddaughter, Alana, almost every night while she was a little girl. Unfortunately, after drinking all that olive oil, the donkey was never the same and it died a few months later. Between the way my father looked at life, and his clever approach to sticky situations, he was never at a loss for a good story. Another had to do with his trips to Naples, where he would go to buy lots of shoes to resell back home in Albania. He knew that if he brought the shoes directly home, he would have to pay import duties, so he devised a foolproof plan. He brought only the left foot shoes back with him. When Albanian customs officials opened his baggage, my father would exclaim, "Look! Those Italians have cheated me! They've sent me home with a worthless shipment of only left foot shoes!" On his next trip, he would bring home the right foot shoes and by this trickery, avoided paying import duties.

While working in my grandfather's thriving business, my father realized that Albanian women wore only black scarves. He thought that we should print our black scarves with different designs and colors and offer prettier choices. My father spoke with my grandpa about his idea, and my grandfather saw the opportunity in the scarves right away. He knew it was worth the risk of spending a little money to produce a line of colorful scarves to see if there was interest. Always creative, my grandfather added floral patterns to the scarves to make them look so much nicer. To produce the patterns, they stamped the ink onto the fabric using flower-embellished stamps.

I was around eight or nine years old when my grandfather began producing scarves with colorful designs. Scarves were the principle way Albanian women had of expressing themselves in public, a tradition that still continues today. It wasn't surprising, then, that colorful scarves would become a big business in Vlora and elsewhere in Albania. We sold countless colored scarves every week in the village market in the center of town, where the vendor carts sold cooked food, fresh produce, flowers, and anything that was available for sale (which wasn't much in those times). My grandmother had a small cart, and she wore a long apron she sewed herself with a single, huge, deep pocket that went all the way from her waist to her feet. We sold our wares from a cart under her watchful eye. I'll never forget how our Nona would sell the scarves from the cart and put the money into that big pocket until it became full of cash. The women who came to buy scarves from our cart loved and respected my grandmother. She was so smart and engaging, and always carried on lively conversations with her customers.

The scarf business quickly grew. Before long, it was as if we had two businesses – scarves and dyeing. That made us happy because we felt we were really serving the community. And in exchange, the community served us. If someone could not afford a scarf, my father would say, "Take it for free." The next day, we would always get baskets of fresh fruit and eggs and all kinds of other things from those same people in return. This elaborate barter system thrived despite the terrible oppression we all lived under. Looking back, it felt like such a nice exchange: people in a community helping one another as best they could during very hard times.

4

FROM GREECE TO ALBANIA

In 1938, Hitler consolidated power in Germany and annexed the Czech Sudetenland and Austria. His growing influence was something all European Jews worried about. Antisemitic rhetoric was becoming common, even accepted, and it was shocking to see that many German people supported this type of hatred. Despite so many fears, somehow life had to continue. In Greece that same year, because of the deteriorating economic conditions, my grandfather Elia's dyeing business (which he shared with his brother Joseph), went bankrupt. They decided it was time to leave Greece, to look for better economic opportunities elsewhere. My uncle Joseph chose to emigrate to Palestine, while my grandfather took an opportunity to help a man in Vlora with his own struggling fabrics business and moved his family to Albania.

In 1939, Italy, under Mussolini, invaded Albania, making the nation its vassal state. Albanian communists and nationalists resisted the Italian occupation through guerrilla warfare, but by 1943, it was apparent that the German Nazis would soon oversee the country, bringing the Holocaust with them. Fearing the worst for her Jewish family – which now included my mother, who had married my father in their traditional Romaniote Jewish community of Ioannina, Greece in 1942, and then moved with him back to Albania – my grandmother appealed to a wealthy Jewish neighbor and friend, Raphael Jakoel, for help in hiding my parents from the Nazis. Jakoel had made his money in real estate and was well connected to the political leaders in Vlora.

Like my parents, Jakoel was originally from Ioannina, but had arrived in Albania much earlier than our family. My grandmother met with him at his fine home in the city and asked him, "Can you find a place for us to hide our son, his wife, and their baby from the Nazis?" She specifically wanted to find a hiding place within Vlora itself, so the family would at least be close together, even in hiding. Jakoel told her he understood her fears, but he was in no position to help her. Some time passed, the situation became more dire and she tried again, this time with much more passion. She pleaded with Jakoel. "Listen," she told him, "I have only this one son. Please help hide him and his family with an Albanian family. If you don't help us, we have no other choice but to go to the mountains and hide with the Muslims. If we go to the mountains, we will need to change our names and become Muslims."

This was an incredible threat for someone in our Jewish community to make. I don't know the reason why Jakoel was unable to help my grandmother, but he rebuffed her again, leaving her with no other options. She visited her dear neighbor and fellow Romaniote Jew Moize Negrin, explained what had happened with Jakoel, and confessed her desperation. Moize Negrin told her that he, his family, and two other Jewish families – the Elia Sollomon and Zoja Joseko families – had plans to leave very soon and take shelter with a close Muslim friend of theirs – Izet Mehmet Lazaj – in a Muslim village called Trevllazër ("Three Brothers") in the mountains nearby. Moize Negrin promised her that he would speak with Izet Mehmet Lazaj once they reached the village, and that he hoped his friend would try to find a Muslim family willing to help.

A short time later, a Muslim man named Kadri Lazaj came on foot to Vlora to collect my family. My parents and grandparents quietly and quickly closed up and left their house and walked with Kadri Lazaj to Trevllazër, bringing only what they could carry. My mother held my brother Elio as they made their way for roughly 20 kilometers (12.5 miles) to the elevations north of Vlora. They walked because there was no transportation to such a place at that time.

Even though it was within reach of Vlora, Trevllazër was a world away. The Muslim villagers were olive oil farmers with small, ancient orchards. They were very poor, living in humble homes that sat close together, providing meager shelter to this condensed and tightly interwoven village of related families. All of this was told to me by Roko Lazaj, Kadri's son, when I visited Trevllazër in November 2012. During my visit, Roko Lazaj took me the very home and room where my parents and grandparents had sheltered. I asked him every question I could think of and recorded videos, trying to capture the feelings that must have enveloped my family as they slipped away into hiding to save their lives.

Kadri and his wife Vera selflessly took in my family. Also living in that home was their grandmother, Anko, and the couple's two children, Dalip and Naile. Later on, they would have more children, but only their son Roko is alive today. Right next door lived Izet Mehmet Lazaj – who was Kadri's cousin – and the Negrin, Sollomon, and Joseko families, who were sheltering with him. Everyone in Trevllazër knew there were "guests" staying in the village and that these guests were Jews. My father gave money to Kadri to buy everyone food. The local imam (the prayer leader of the mosque), Musa Sinani, gave everyone in my family a Muslim first name. My grandfather became "Muhamet," my grandmother became "Fatima," my father became "Daut," my mother became "Bule," and my brother Elio became "Ali."

Roko told me that my family spent five to seven months hiding in Trevllazër. My parents always said they spent six months there. We know that German occupation of Albania occurred between September 1943 and November 1944, so this would certainly have been the most dangerous time for Albanian Jews. The village turned out to be very safe and no one betrayed those in hiding. My grandparents and parents lived quite comfortably and harmoniously with the villagers, who accepted them as their own. They didn't have to hide in holes or walls or attics, or feel taken advantage of, or suffer degradations – or even worry that they were imposing on their gracious Muslim hosts. They were made to feel completely welcome. Even after the war ended and they returned to their home in Vlora, my family remained friends with the Muslims who had so kindly and unconditionally sheltered them in Trevllazër.

I did not grow up hearing stories about this period of hiding, however. After the war ended and it was safe for Jews to return to their homes, Albania came under communist rule that continued for nearly 50 years. In the aftermath of World War II, even in Albania where Jews had been protected, those who had been hidden or allowed Jews to hide among them spoke not a word of it. Still living under oppression, with religion outlawed and religious practices forbidden, the stories of heroic hidings of the Jewish people were simply swept under the rug. Life went on for many, many years without giving proper recognition to these selfless saviors of the Jewish people.

As a child who knew nothing of my parents' and grandparents' and older brother's secret past, when I was five or six years old something finally happened to bring what they had gone through to my attention. My mother and I were walking on the street in Vlora when we heard someone shouting, "Bule! Bule!" My mom turned around, and a young lady her age hurried up to us. Right away, she and my mother began hugging and exchanging kisses like long lost sisters. I could not understand why the woman called my mother "Bule" since I knew that was not her name. They were hugging and kissing and crying and I just watched in complete confusion.

As we walked home after this strange encounter, my mother explained to me that during the German occupation of Albania, she and my father and Grandpa Elia and Grandma Anetta had gone into hiding in Trevllazër and had lived there as Muslims. She told me about the village, the family they lived with, and the simple life they led while in hiding. She said the village produced fresh fruit and vegetables, and was of course known for its olive oil. I marveled at the story of their secret life in the mountains and their pretend names. At my young age, it all seemed like a dream to me, and such a change from their lives in Vlora!

My parents had earned a good reputation in the little mountain town and were well respected by everyone. After all, they truly were good-hearted people. They were always eager to help those in need, and people loved them for that. My parents were strong role models who bolstered my natural instincts for helping others, an attitude I have had throughout my life. Roko's stories corroborated what my parents had told me about their time in hiding. I continue to this day to try and gain recognition for the Lazaj family from Yad Vashem for what they did. Unfortunately, the people who make these decisions have told me there is not yet enough documentation. This is the dilemma of having to suppress the truth about this period under Hoxha's communist regime after the war. But I will never stop trying to bring our family's saviors the recognition they deserve.

Back in Vlora, my family's kind-heartedness did not detract in any way from their keen business sense. After the war, their scarf dyeing business would be looked upon as at the leading edge of a fashion trend that brought an end to the bleak traditional black garb of the Eastern European lower classes. What's more, they managed to accomplish this fashion revolution even in the years of extreme Albania hardship during the grip of the communist dictatorship. Every day, people would come to our house because they knew we were selling colored scarves and that we could dye their clothes. Many of them were not able to pay in cash, and they would offer fresh eggs or milk from their farms instead. We never turned anyone away. Because of this, we always maintained a great relationship with the people of Vlora. Everyone paid something because they were respectful and did not want to insult us by asking for something for free. And so, through loyal relationships and barter, we managed to have a nice life even through the darkest times. We had everything we needed while the rest of the population was poor and nearly starving. Bartering with our community was how we made our living.

Decades later in 2006 when I was named an honorary citizen of Vlora, with the help of the Albanian Ministry of Foreign Affairs, I officially had the name of the street where we lived changed to "The Jewish Street," to honor the Jewish families who had lived there in the communist era, including our own. I also had a plaque made with the names of all the Jewish families inscribed on it. The street sign and plaque were installed in Vlora during a touching ceremony, and it's something I am very proud of.

During the Jewish holidays in Vlora, when I was growing up, all the Jews would come out of their houses dressed beautifully – the men in their best suits and the women in their most colorful dresses. Everybody in town would stare at us dressed in our finest clothes, which made us feel so beautiful and special. In my mind as a young girl, I felt all the Jews I knew were beautiful, and that everybody in our community was attractive and wealthy. It made me think that there were no poor Jews in the world at all.

Later when I visited Israel as an adult, my ideas about what it meant to be a Jew and what Jews were like were upended. In Israel, I was disheartened to see that many Jews were very poor. In my imagination as a Jewish child born and brought up in a well-off Jewish family in Albania – a poor country to begin with – I thought if we had a good life, then all Jews everywhere had good lives. But of course, I would learn that just wasn't so.

5

MUSLIM SAVIORS

I have spoken often over the years about my family's struggles during World War II, how my Jewish family immigrated from Greece to Albania, and spent many months hiding in an Albanian Muslim village for safety during the German occupation of Albania. Because the Muslims hid my family, my grandparents and parents were not captured and executed by the Germans. Those kind people saved the lives of my loved ones, and as a direct consequence, they made my life possible.

And as I also mentioned, even though they had been in hiding, my parents did not tell my siblings and I much about their saviors. It's important to understand that after the war Albania became a repressive communist country. Religion was persecuted and it suddenly became dangerous to reveal that you had hidden Jews (or gone into hiding yourself) during the war. The communist government (which was finally overthrown in 1990, making Albania the last European nation to expel its communist regime), tried to pretend that Jews did not exist in Albania. Hoxha ended religious freedom, destroyed synagogues, and slaughtered people of all religions. He particularly targeted Christian and Muslim clerics, imprisoning some leaders for decades and killing many others.

The people of Albania had been exceptionally welcoming to Jews all through their history, but especially when the Nazis invaded and occupied the country in 1943. Albania was known for religious tolerance and many diverse groups lived for years in peace and harmony. Albania was a haven, if there ever was one, for Jews during that terrible time. It is said that Albert Einstein traveled to the US in April 1933 using an Albanian passport. More importantly, Albania was the only occupied nation in Europe where there were more Jews after the war than before it. Virtually every Albanian Jew survived. Much of that resulted from the selfless acts of rescuers among the Albanian Muslim and Christian populations, who should be credited with turning Albania into what people called "The Garden of Eden" for Jewish refugees during the Holocaust.

After Hoxha and the communists took over the country, an Albanian man who saved Jews was thrown in jail for having done so. When my father heard about that, he did not want anything to happen to the people who saved our family, so he kept the whole ordeal a complete secret, even from us children. We just didn't know much about what had really happened.

Years later, every time I would travel to Albania, I was always curious to find out more about the people who saved my family. I eventually got in touch with political leaders in Vlora and asked for their help. They investigated, asking older people what they knew of the village and the story. Eventually, during my 2012 visit to Albania for the 100th anniversary of Albanian independence (which I attended as a guest of the government), they told me they had found the Muslim family that helped my parents and grandparents. It was then that I first learned the names Kadri and Vera Lazaj.

Unfortunately, by the time I received this news, the Lazajs were long dead, but during that visit to Albania, I decided I wanted to meet anyone still living who was related to them. I had some Albanian friends go to the village, seek out a relative and let them know that I wanted to meet them. As a result of this, I was able to meet Kadri and Vera's son, Roko. He and his grandchildren were carrying on the traditions of olive oil farming in Trevllazër. He took me to the old house where my parents lived while in hiding, which was now vacant and in disrepair. It was beyond moving for me to step into the home and exact room where my family had hidden. I imagined them arriving to this strange place, adopting new names, and living among the Muslim villagers. I asked Roko why the house was not in use or had not been rebuilt. He told me he had simply decided to build a new house on the other side of his land, but that he'd left the old house standing.

Albanian Muslims in another village close to Vlora were also known to have saved Jews from the Nazis and I have sought to identify those people so they, too, can be honored by Yad Vashem. But so far, the necessary documentation has fallen short of proving their humanitarian acts, though I have no doubt at all about what they did.

There are other harrowing stories about our family from that era. During the communist years, which began in 1944, intellectuals were jailed, and many others found themselves harassed and followed, their lives in great jeopardy. One of them was my uncle Shemo Kohen, my father's brother-in-law who had married and left Greece much earlier than my family. Uncle Shemo was living in southern Albania and had a thriving fabrics business and a beautiful house. When the Germans came, he went into hiding. The Germans commandeered his house and used it as a headquarters. At the end of the war, they decided to destroy the military intelligence they were leaving behind, so they blew up the house. A rain of bricks and gold coins blanketed the street. Shemo, after all, had been very wealthy. In 1955, during the communist rule, someone spied on Shemo and told the Sigurimi i Shtetit that he and my father were in possession of a treasure trove of gold coins. My younger brother, Abe, and I remember everything that happened, just as if it were yesterday. Dressed in dark suits, the Sigurimi i Shtetit came to our house. With guns in their hands, they took my uncle and my father out to the courtyard, made them face the wall, and yelled at them over and over, "We know you have gold coins! Where did you bury them? We will shoot you if you don't tell us!" Abe and I watched this happen, looking down from the second story of our home.

My father answered that they had no gold coins. But my uncle got scared and told them the gold was hidden inside the well in the middle of our courtyard. So, the Sigurimi i Shtetit ordered my mother and my uncle's maid, Fani Kabeli, to get buckets and empty the well. The two women pulled up bucket after bucket of water to empty the well and when they were done, the gold was found buried in the wall of the well and dug out. As my brother and I watched, a container was removed from the well that looked to us like a large sombrero. Once opened, it was revealed that the case was indeed filled with gold. My father was very upset with Shemo because some of those gold coins were his, too. But they had their lives. The communist regime kept Albania isolated from other countries for almost 50 years and stole not just gold from its people, but freedom, safety, and worst of all, hope.

6

ALL IN THE FAMILY

Every member of my family, from grandparents to grandchildren, pitched in to help make our clothes dyeing and colorful scarves business work. We were all expected to share the many duties and tasks, which meant that when school was out of session in the summertime, we children were required to work at home before playtime or fun could begin. My father was the primary labor enforcer, but Grandma Anetta was our commander in chief.

In the summer months we would rent a modest house on a beautiful Vlora beach so we could enjoy some time away from school and our lives in town. We'd venture to the oasis of our beach house in the afternoons, returning to town in the early mornings to do our usual labors. Renting a summer beach house was commonly done among those with even moderately successful businesses in Vlora.

All through the summer break, grandma roused us from sleep at 4:00 a.m. and put us to work until 7:00 a.m. My younger brother Abe – who my father called "Little Shrewdy" – and I would stumble out of bed at the alarm clock's bell, travel back into town, and spend the next hours stamping flowers onto scarves using stencils and ink. Elio, the oldest of us four Kohen children, was excused because of his studies and his privileged position as the eldest child. My father would tell Abe and I, "When the ink runs out, your work is done." That simple lesson kept us all going until our task was completely finished and served us well in our work ethics in life.

To be raised by adults who were savvy in business and clever in life rubbed off on us in more ways than one. As kids often do, we sometimes wished our early morning workdays would go a little faster. We knew we would be done when our dye ran out. To speed up the draining of the ink for our stencils, we would take the dye bottles and pour some of the dye into the ashes of the family hearth where it wouldn't be noticed. When Pop saw how little dye we had left in our bottles, he would proclaim that we had worked hard enough and send us off to the beach.

The ruse worked perfectly the few times that we tried it. But really, most of the time my siblings and I worked very hard and gave up a lot of summer vacation and sleep before we could join our friends at the beach. When people asked how we could spend our summer days playing at the beach and enjoying a big, rented house without having to work, my grandmother would vehemently defend us. If they said that our family was lucky to enjoy such a life of leisure when others around us could not, my grandmother would say to them, "These kids are up at four o'clock in the morning. They are working hard while you are sleeping. These are working kids and they deserve everything they have. They earned it."

We were very fortunate to belong to the almost nonexistent middle class in those communist days in Vlora – amid widespread poverty. For our contributions to the business, our parents rewarded us with spending money that we used to buy simple things like ice cream. Between working in the family business, and school, and what little bit of leisure time we could manage, it never really occurred to us to quarrel with each other. I got along quite well with my siblings. At the age of eight or so, I remember the four of us eating at our own little table, with ages ranging from around ten down to about four. We sat in our chairs and ate together very nicely. We very much loved each other, and we really were a happy family.

I also recall, however, that my younger brother, Abe, was a bit more rambunctious than the rest of us. Abe craved attention. And like me, he was very close to our grandmother. Sometimes Abe would fold his arms and say, "I'm not eating," while the rest of us were busy eating everything put on our plates. The adults would try everything to get Abe to eat; they would even make him French fries, which was a rare treat in those days.

This sparked our entrepreneurial spirits, and Abe and I decided to embark upon a mutually advantageous business exchange. When no one from the adult table was looking or paying any attention to our kids' table, I would buy his French fries with money I had saved. I wanted those good, tasty fries, but they hadn't been put on my plate. He took my money and the deal worked out for both of us. This arrangement continued for some time, and no one was the wiser (or if the adults knew, they never let on).

Then there was another young boy, a Jewish neighbor named Leon Sareta – we called him "Lonja" – who I plotted with in a scheme involving ice cream. The shop that sold ice cream was a few blocks away, and sometimes I was too lazy to go to buy it for myself, so I would send Lonja. I would call out from our doorway, "Lonja! Lonja!" and he'd come running to me from where he was playing. I'd tell him to go buy me some ice cream and I'd give him enough money to also buy a cone for himself. And he would run to the store, but then on the way home, he would sometimes forget the deal and come back licking both cones. I'd say, "Lonja! What did you do? You ate my ice cream!" Then I would send him back for a fresh cone. I think I was ten at that time and he must have been six or seven.

Being a child in communist Albania, a tiny third world nation by any definition, meant existing in political and other situations that were completely different from anything experienced by children in Western nations. There were many oppressions and difficulties. But despite all, it is impossible to say that there were no good times. Children are resilient and we had fun as kids. No, we didn't have any toys or luxuries. If we wanted to play with a ball, we had to make one from wound up pieces of yarn. I made my own dolls and became very good at constructing them. As kids, we knew how to invent things because even though we had spending money, there just wasn't much we could buy. Still, we were happy because we just didn't know any different, such was our life in Albania.

One thing we didn't understand as kids, however, was the stress our parents lived with because of the Hoxha dictatorship. My childhood in Vlora was not much different than it might have been for any child my age in any country. In fact, my life in those days seemed to closely resemble a child's life in small town America. Kids from Brooklyn to Nebraska would recognize how we played together and teased one another. After school, I would walk to my friend Cela's house, and we would play hopscotch in her garden. My father's rule was that I had to return home before sunset, and that is what I always did. In the evenings, my siblings and I attended to our studies after dinner. This was the daily routine during our formative years.

One exception was Elio, my older brother, and the oldest child in the family. For him, the afternoons were slightly different than for the rest of us. He was gifted in math, and very good looking. Every afternoon after school, several beautiful girls would come by the house asking for Elio because they knew he would be there doing his math homework. They would sit at our table with him. And what were they after? Well, let's just say that Elio, the math whiz, became very good at doing those pretty girls' schoolwork for them.

But Elio was much more than just his good looks and brains. He was known to be handy, athletic, and something of a showoff. For example, on those rare occasions when it snowed in Vlora, Elio liked to go outside wearing nothing but his tiny European bathing suit. He'd sit down in the cold and cover himself in snow, presumably waiting for high school girls to wander by and noticed him! And my younger brother, Abe, had his own cold weather ritual. Since it didn't snow that often, he liked to get dressed in winter clothes and then stand in front of a mirror practicing his smile. I remember his vanity act clearly and I'll never forget those looks he would make at himself in the mirror. He'd stand there posing until he found the smile he wanted to use. Then he'd go the local photographer's studio – we didn't own cameras back then – and have his picture taken with snow on his shoulders. Abe was a character then and is to this day. I still have his snow day pictures in my photo album.

After our busy days filled with work, studies, and play, bedtime came for the Kohen children as it does for all young kids. And like children the world over, we wanted to hear bedtime stories. Since the adults in our family were either too worn out or still at work, the task of delivering these stories fell to me. We didn't own many children's books, so I would dream up tall tales for my siblings each night. I have no idea how I made something up night after night, but all these many years later my younger siblings, Abe and Alice, both remember those silly stories I used to tell.

During my high school years, I had two close friends, Eli and Cela. The three of us were inseparable, and we spent countless hours together hanging out and enjoying ourselves in town. One day, we found out that the local Catholic church was preparing a free food event. We figured we might as well go and see what it was all about. So, there we were – a Jewish girl, a Muslim girl, and a Christian Greek Orthodox girl – and the three of us went to the Catholic church, where we ate plenty of food and had lots of fun. Sure enough, the next day we went to school and found out that somebody had spied on us – as was common then, because the country was under communist rule – and told our principal what we did. At that time, you were not allowed to go to church, even though some of the churches were still open. As a punishment, he made the three of us stand in front of the entire school, which included 1st grade all the way up to 11th grade and announced, "See these three girls. They were in the church, and this is against what we believe in." They made us feel like we were nothing. I was so humiliated, I wanted to bury myself under the earth. Upset and crying, we stood in front of the whole school as our principal made an example of us. These were the kinds of things that the communists did and there was nothing anyone could do about it. They used fear to keep everyone in line. After that experience, the three of us never went back to any church again for any reason. Our classmates followed suit as well, afraid that if they went to church the same thing would happen to them. It was so cruel to use kids in this way, but it worked. I knew well that the Hoxha government was responsible for what happened to me that day, and I never forgot it.

Even with the communists in power, or possibly *because* the communists were in power, Albanians always seemed to rally around each other. Religious differences, particularly among schoolmates, were irrelevant. At the time, this country of three million had a Jewish population of perhaps just a few hundred people. Nearly a quarter of Albanians were Greek Orthodox. The rest were Muslim, but under communism, religious practice of any kind was strictly forbidden. Teenagers at that time did not care whether they dated a Christian, a Jew, or a Muslim. If anything good arose from communism, it was that everyone was considered equal – and lived equally poor lives – and religion did not separate us. Interfaith marriages were common. And when holidays came around, we celebrated all of them – from Ramadan to Easter – every holiday was outlawed, but Albanians love to celebrate, so we made a point of celebrating our own holidays and also our neighbors'. Many years later, this harmony still exists between religions in Albania, even despite the terrible internecine wars and genocides that have occurred in neighboring countries like Serbia, Bosnia, and Croatia. The one possible exception to this egalitarianism, I would say, came from Jewish parents who in their hearts wanted their children to find and marry within the faith. But with such a tiny Jewish population, finding a suitable partner among other Jews was very difficult and, as a result, many married outside the religion.

There were some who resorted to abandoning their principles and joining the Communist Party because it allowed them to go to university or to ease their poverty, even though they did not believe in the corrupt system. Some who did this were given good positions in government. But the price was steep. They had to pledge their allegiance to Communism and proclaim their belief in the dictator. There was a huge picture of Stalin by the bank in the center of Vlora, and I remember that when Stalin died, many people actually cried. It was 1953 and I was just eight years old, but I remember clearly that I was upset and cried for Stalin. That's how brainwashed we were by the propaganda in our schools. Looking back, it seems utterly crazy.

I have a friend from Poland who is my age. One day, as we were discussing our childhoods, I asked her whether she cried when Stalin died. She said, "Of course we did. We all did."

As children in Eastern Europe, we had no real idea or understanding of the terrible systems we were living in, or how our parents suffered under this type of oppression.

7

FAMILY TRADITIONS

My family chiefly followed the traditions of Greece, the country of my parent's birth. But after my grandparents and father moved to Albania, they adopted the Albanian traditions, which bear similarities to those in Greece. We observed the Jewish holidays that, of course, transcend national borders. And when it came to our family traditions, we had plenty of our own. Every holiday, my grandma would spend the entire day cooking for us, creating special dishes that we didn't have every day. Indeed, she was always in the kitchen planning and providing for us. Sometimes she would take my siblings and I on the bus to the beach, which was about a 45-minute ride back then. (Today it's only about ten minutes.) We'd look at the beautiful water, the houses, and the boats, and then come back home on the same bus. This was her way of getting away from everything that she did for us at home. Other days she would take me by the hand and say that we were going for a bus ride, just the two of us. Riding the bus was great entertainment for her, like taking a tour. She wanted to relax, I guess, and I loved to accompany her. I felt so lucky to be her companion, and we did it quite often. It was our own special treat.

Nona and I also spent time together on the boulevard, about a 15-minute walk from home. The boulevard at the center of the city was the hub of the town. People walked about with their families and greeted each other, catching up on neighborhood news and gossip. There was a *lulishte*, a beautiful flower garden, and tables where you could sit. People would bring in their own food, like chicken and potatoes, to be cooked in a special oven and it would be ready at the end of the day. Most people didn't have an oven at home, so the ovens on the boulevard were a needed service. Then they would eat their food at the tables like they were at a restaurant. The only requirement was to buy some lemonade or a cold drink. It was our way of having fun and it didn't really cost anything.

At home we had a wood-burning stove. More often than not, grandma cooked for the family on that stove. She specialized in casseroles, soups, and other dishes, but cooking was far from the only thing she could do well. She was also a very smart and shrewd businesswoman, making plenty of money selling our scarves from her cart in the market.

Private automobiles were rare in Albania, and the cars on the streets were nearly always government-owned vehicles. Bicycles were not as rare, but still they were a special luxury, especially good ones. One time, my older brother, Elio, won a very nice bicycle in a lottery. It was such a big deal that it seemed like every kid in the city came to see his bicycle and ask him if they could ride it. He was so proud that he won this bicycle. I, however, never got a bike for myself. I was a klutz. I tried to ride but couldn't do it. Decades later, despite traveling the world and living in New York City for years, I have never learned to ride a bike.

While the Western world, when in need of food, clothing, or almost anything else, is accustomed to simply going to a store to shop, in communist Albania such shopping was impossible. Instead, there were outdoor markets, similar to modern farmers' markets. This was where those who could shop hoped to find what they needed. It was in these markets where Anetta asserted herself at sales, very much to her advantage. She was somehow different from everyone else in the Vlora market. She would say to the vendors, "Okay, give me your freshest tomatoes." So, we would have the freshest fruit and vegetables because they knew her and knew she wasn't kidding around. They were a little afraid of her, too. They knew she was a good buyer, and that she would find a way to pick the best of everything they had to use in the wonderful meals she cooked for our family. They all respected her because she was very special like that. I think maybe it was because she treated people with love. She was a giver who was good to people. I think they liked her also because she was Jewish. Most Albanians liked Jews because they thought we were smart, and they respected our history.

In that era, most Albanians living in the larger towns and cities were educated people, primarily because education was a priority of the government. However, this did not translate to advanced or higher education, which was reserved mostly for the elite class and Communist Party members. Basic schooling was provided for free by the government, but for a variety of reasons many families did not send their children to school at all, which produced a largely illiterate populace, particularly in the small villages and rural areas.

8

FAMILY LIFE

For as much as I loved and admired my father, the greatest hero of my life was my grandmother, Anetta. She raised us. I was lucky to have had an educated grandmother. She'd studied and finished at the Alliance Française in Ioannina at a time when women did not go to school. She raised us differently than most. She was so smart, and always shared her life experiences with us through her stories. Other grandmothers in our region weren't as educated, didn't know much about the world outside Albania, and didn't have a diversity of interests. Our grandmother was able to teach us about business, about running a household, how to cook, and how to be a powerful person in a challenging world. We were very well behaved because of her and she also saw to it that we did well in school. My grandmother was a very strong woman, very powerful. Occasionally I faced bullying in school, but if I said to my oppressor, "Don't come near me or I'm going to call my grandma!" that was enough to scare them off. That's how strong she was. She wasn't a big person physically, but she had a huge persona. Given the opportunity, my grandmother could have become anything she wanted to be. Her brother, who was ten years younger than her, became a doctor; she easily could have done the same, but in those days women were not encouraged to pursue advanced education. When she came to Albania, she lost the opportunities she may have had back in Ioannina, few as they were. But even in Greece, most women only did housework and their schooling often ended quite young. After my first cousin, Eni, finished high school in Albania, all her friends went on to college – but her father didn't permit this, and she was soon a married housewife.

In Vlora, one type of activity known to bring together many families was a big picnic. We loved going to the picnics, and they always felt like such a production. To give back to the community through these events, my father and mother would often take poor families to the picnic, too. This was their way of using some of the good fortune they found in business to help others. Sometimes my parents would put us all on a truck and we would go to the little village nearby called Nartë, about three or four miles away. Nartë was known for grapes and its winery, and so as soon as we arrived, we would cut some grapes and eat them. Nartë was not so far away, but it was very different from our lives in Vlora. We always had so much fun and the picnic events were a very special way to enjoy time with family, friends, and neighbors.

As I mentioned before, my handsome father, with his charm and wit, had women standing in line every Sunday, waiting for him to read their coffee cups. In the rings of coffee grounds at the bottom of their cups, he'd search for clues about the future (something he'd done since he was a young man). With Greek or Turkish coffee, after drinking the hot liquid one would place the saucer upside down on top of the cup, then (after performing a little ritual) flip the cup and saucer over, with the cup now resting upside down on the saucer. After a few minutes, the fortune-teller would separate the cup and saucer and read the fortune based on how the grounds and liquid appeared on both. My father liked being a fortune-teller, it was fun for him. He did it to liven things up in Vlora where there was nothing else to do except go to the movies. Reading the coffee cups was real comedy and my father was the comedian. My mother was much more serious, but she loved to sing and dance – traits that I inherited from her.

My grandfather also had a serious side. An educated man who

read Hebrew, he made sure that the family took our holidays seriously, particularly Passover, when he spent time meticulously reading the Haggadah in full and in Hebrew. Like most, however, he had his flaws. He was known to drink and smoke, which could lead to occasional displays of bad temper. On these nights, as we all sat together at the table, if the kids made any type of noise, he would get very upset. If he got too incensed, he would yank the tablecloth away, causing the dishes to crash to the floor and break. You might say he was an alcoholic, but it was hard to tell because in those days so many of the adults drank. The drink of course, was Albanian raki, which was so strong. It was common for men to gather in cafes and bars to drink, smoke, and play cards or *Shesh Besh,* a Turkish form of backgammon.

Most times, my Grandpa Elia handled family discipline with a gentle manner. He was very nice to my siblings and me, except those few times when he wanted quiet and respect such as during the Jewish holidays – and he wasn't kidding about this. My siblings and I would be at our kids' table with our aunt's children. Sometimes, like kids do, we would start giggling, but he let us know when we were crossing the line.

Considering our perfect storm of living under harsh authoritarian rule in a country with a poor infrastructure and economy, along with an inadequate healthcare system, it is not surprising that life expectancy in Albania in the mid-1960s was only about 65 years. By the time he turned 70, my grandfather was bedridden. He was very sick, but his doctor told him that he should get out of bed and walk a bit. And guess whose job it was to get him out of bed and make him walk – me! I was young, but I would pull him up and say to him, "Come on, Papu, let's get up and walk." And he would walk along slowly. I was able to get him to do this difficult task that he didn't want to do himself. He didn't go to the doctor, and I don't remember what he was ailing from, but at this stage in his life he was sick all the time.

I remember much less about my mother from those days, probably because she left the house very early in the morning and worked long hours at her job at the port of Vlora. My father worked there as well, as an accountant. We listened to our mother when she gave us instructions, but she was not home so much of the time. For that reason, my grandmother Anetta was by far my most significant female influence and was in practice the dominant figure in the Kohen household. Anetta was home all day, cooking and cleaning, and she ran the house.

My grandmother and my mother got along well enough, but somewhat out of necessity more than choice. We all lived together. When my mom left Greece, she had nobody in Albania but my father, and so she was totally alone. That's how it was in Albania, you lived with your in-laws. In my mother's case, she was at least able to work outside the home while my grandma took care of the household and the four kids.

My grandmother had a close relationship with my father, her son. She also had two daughters in Greece, both older than my father, and both who managed to survive the war. But in Albania a son is special because he is expected to take over leadership of the family. Daughters were valueless in those days. The interesting thing is that after we left Albania, my cousin Pepo heard stories about how I helped my father in business, and he said, "Wow! We did not know that Eni (my nickname) was David's 'son.' All this time we thought that one of David's sons was doing what she did for her father." They could not believe that a daughter – not a son – stepped in and helped the way I did. To me, everything I did felt natural. And in the back of my mind, I did it all to make my father proud of me.

None of the other Jewish girls I knew would have been recognized by their fathers as being more capable than their brothers, even if they were. In that way, I was lucky to have the father that I did. Even though our family had money, almost everyone was poor in Vlora. But I didn't see poverty when I looked at my Jewish girlfriends, I saw only beauty.

The greatest satisfaction of my life has been the fulfillment of my dreams, both personally and professionally. People have often said that my accomplishments were due to luck, given when I was born and where I came from. But I believe that if you want to do something, and you work hard, you can make your dreams come true. It's not luck at all. It's hard work and perseverance.

My "hard-work-comes-first" attitude is at least a partial reflection of my Grandma Anetta. My father and my brother Elio used to tell me that I was just like Nona. Elio didn't always like the way our grandma treated my mother, so he was always on our mother's side. But I was too young to understand that. He was two-and-a-half years older than me. Now my little granddaughter is just like me. I don't know if that's good or bad, but the world will find out soon enough.

9

SCHOOL OR SHIDDUCH

By the time my siblings and I were tweens and teens, people began to tell my mother that her children were strikingly beautiful. They called us "The Flowers of Vlora" and said that we brought sunshine everywhere we went. I never thought of myself in this way, I was just being me. But I did notice that when the four of us lined up (each two years apart), we made quite an impression with our chiseled Greek features, thick manes of hair, and confident smiles. Throughout our childhoods, we seemed to blossom like flowers, soaking up excitement like the sun, and bringing enthusiasm to every event we took part in. We had serene expressions, dancing eyes, and unbounding energy, which we had been raised and encouraged to exude by our charismatic parents and grandparents. The attention was flattering (and also a little embarrassing). I was sheltered and innocent, obeyed my parents, and worked hard in school and for the family business. It was nice to be compared to a flower: delicate and beautiful, growing instinctively, and with a unique flare. And by now, I was also approaching the age at which some Albanian girls got married.

Marriage was not something that was on my mind even though it had been joked about since I was a young girl. I remember during the Jewish holidays at our rabbi Isak Koen's house, his grown daughter

39

would talk with my father and say that her son, Zino, and I should be married. I was perhaps ten years old at the time and Zino was only a few years older. I was so embarrassed by the conversation that I hid under the table. In 1959, when I turned 14, gentile Albanian families began to come to our house a few times a year wanting to make a marriage match with me and their sons. I found it all utterly embarrassing; I couldn't imagine being told to marry at that tender age. Luckily, my father turned these families away, telling them that I was still too young.

No matter what their family's religion or customs were, teenagers in Albania had social lives not unlike their counterparts in the West, despite the strictly enforced social behavior. Undaunted by the rules, my high school classmates and I attended parties throughout the school year. But make no mistake, socializing could only take place in secret. No girl had an "official" boyfriend whose hand she could hold in public. If we were to go steady with someone, especially for the girls, we had to do it in secret because dating was frowned upon by our society. It wasn't very hard to find a boyfriend, but the custom was that parents would marry off their kids through family ties and arrangements. For us Jews, we had something called *shidduch* – Jewish matchmaking. As I grew older into my teen years and shidduch became more of a possibility for me, I told my father I was not interested in getting married. I explained that I was too young, and that I wanted to continue my studies. I was very clear about this because education was my goal. My dream was to become a doctor, so my plan was to go through school and not fall in love until after I graduated.

This, however, did not turn out to be the case. When I turned 17, my grandmother and her best friend, Eleni Shamo, hoped to fix me up with Eleni's brother's son – her nephew, Theodore. Eleni's brother was a very famous doctor, tall and handsome, and everyone in his family spoke Greek like our family did. That summer, Eleni brought her nephew to our house and introduced him to me. He was 22, and very good looking. He was tall, well dressed, and had blue eyes. His fine clothing came from Greece, where his family had relatives who sent them nice things they could not otherwise get in Albania.

His nickname was Dhori, short for Theodore. Of course, he called me Eni like everyone else, but when he said it, it sounded different, like I was *his* Eni. Though his family lived in Vlora, he was attending dental school in Tirana. I loved him from the first time I saw him. When he came home to Vlora in the summers, we would gather a lot of young people our age, our friends and cousins, and take the public bus to a secret beach that we would have all to ourselves. We would scramble down rocks to get to the sandy shore from the road, where the Adriatic waters before us would be breathtakingly deep and blue. We would swim, sing together, and go out on rowboats, enjoying the summer sun and the water in a gorgeous, picturesque scene.

Dhori was my secret fiancé for almost two-and-a-half years. During that time, we were never alone, and of course never had even one intimate moment. This was forbidden before marriage, and we followed the rules our parents set for us. Later, when I was 18 and started medical school in Tirana, Dhori and I would meet in secret at his sister's apartment. It was 1965. He was in the third year of his DDS dental program, and I was in my first year of medical school, which I would soon change to dental school because of his influence. We would meet every Tuesday, my day off from school. There, I would teach him French, and we would kiss and hold each other, but nothing more. We cherished our secret rendezvous, but we were still like innocent children.

I did not have family to stay with in Tirana and so I lived in a student dormitory at the university. It wasn't unusual for a woman to attend university in Albania at that time, nor to go on to have a professional career. But it was unusual for a student to not have family support nearby. Luckily for me, there were two Jewish families that I could visit and rely on, the Matathias and the Jakoels. Mrs. Jakoel – her given name was Fortuni – took me to her room the first time I visited and gave me a drawer in her dresser that had a lock. She told me, "This drawer is for you. Put all your valuables and cash here and I will always keep them safe." She and her husband, Isaak, were both Holocaust survivors, though they had not been married during the war. Along with her first husband, Fortuni had been rounded up by the Nazis in Preveza, Greece, in 1944, where the young couple (newlyweds of just six months) were living. Fortuni survived the Nazi concentration camps, but her husband did not. She weighed less than 70 pounds when she was liberated. She made her way back to her husband's family in Greece, but without him, she discovered she was no longer welcome there. She returned to her own parents in Albania, Aneta and Elia Vituli, who owned a liquor store in the southern town of Gjirokastra. They were utterly overjoyed because they thought she was dead. Eventually, she married Isaak, who had lost his wife and two children to the Nazis. Together, Fortuni and Isaak went on to have three children, and I became good friends with their daughter, Zhana. During the Jewish holidays I would go with them to the home of Chaim Batino for the services, which of course were done in secret. The other Jewish family I knew in Tirana, the Matathias, were supportive of me, but they were the parents of Zino, whom they had wanted me to marry since I was ten years old. I had to let him down because I thought of him like a brother, and besides, Zino wasn't all that interested in me anyway. Back when Zino's younger brother, Isaak, was born the family was living in Vlora. Zino and Isaak's mother, Hrisi, couldn't produce milk, so my mother had breastfed baby Isaak. Aside from those two families, my cousin Enni and her family also lived near Tirana in Kavaja. Since I was not an Albanian citizen, I needed official permission from the police to travel anywhere, so I could not easily visit them. I often felt upset about our lack of freedoms in Albania, even just to travel from town to town to see our friends and family required approval.

As a medical student, I had plenty of schoolwork to do and spent most of my time at my dormitory. The building had three levels: the top floor was for female students, the second floor for males, and the main floor was the cafeteria and library. We slept on bunk beds, six girls to a room, and my room was in the corner of the building. Though it was forbidden, some of us had electric appliances to cook with, and after the dormitory director went home for the day, we would make simple meals together in our rooms. Our contraband appliances often made the power in our room go out, but luckily, we had an electrician on duty – me! I knew how to change fuses and flip the circuit breakers and things like that. I was also the hairdresser, and the organizer of our secret fashions shows. None of this sort of fun was allowed, but we managed to break the rules secretly late at night. At Christmastime, we'd always decorate a tree together, called the *Pema e vitit te Ri*, "The New Year's Tree." This was located near the library and allowed by the school since it was not religious. Outside our window, the young men from the floor below would often serenade us, and sometimes we would have to throw water down on them to get them to stop. Next door to my room were two girls, one from Ghana and another from Cameroon, both studying at our university. I was very good friends with them and loved learning about their lives in Africa. Life in the dormitory was so much fun!

I enjoyed living in the dorm and had much fun with the girls who lived there, but at the same time I also felt somewhat separated from them and my other classmates. Because my family had come from Greece and had not become Albanian citizens, I was still considered a foreigner even though I had been born in the country. And because my family had money, I wasn't given the scholarship that Albanian students typically received, and my father had to pay for everything. My beautiful clothes from Greece made me stand out as well, so I soon gave them away and went back to wearing my black high school uniform so I would not be singled out or treated badly by jealous teachers or students. I was not allowed to eat for free in the cafeteria, as my dormmates and classmates were, and during the weekly *Zbor* exercises – required military training for all Albanian citizens – I was not allowed to attend, so at this time each week I would also be alone. On the training mornings I would wait at my window until I saw Dhori walking across the campus. I really could not even think straight until I set my eyes on him. I was insecure because he was so good looking and had such a great sense of humor. So many pretty girls liked him. Compared to them, I had no romantic experience. My upbringing was quite traditional and sheltered – in fact, as a young woman I was only allowed to leave the house with my older brother, Elio, who served as my protector. I worried that Dhori did not love me as much as I loved him, even though he promised me that he did.

As our relationship grew, Dhori's family began to treat me as someone of importance. When his father died after a long illness, I served the coffee for the family, a position usually reserved for a new bride. This was a clear indication of where I stood with them.

In addition, it felt safe to be in love with Dhori. From the first time we met, I knew if my grandmother was going to make the shidduch match for me, it meant that she knew he was the one. Dhori became my true love. I thought about him when I woke up, all during the day, and when I went to bed at night. I loved him and wanted to spend my life with him. When I was beside him, I was very proud to have such a smart and handsome boyfriend. And in turn, he made me feel so beautiful. He respected me as a woman and that time was one of the most passionately wonderful periods of my life.

But before we could marry, my father concocted a scheme to allow my family to emigrate from Albania, and emigration would mean leaving Dhori behind. I couldn't bear the thought of losing my Dhori! We were already planning our lives together, and this would completely change everything. But from the moment my father shared his intention to escape Hoxha's prison of a nation, I saw the writing on the wall. I knew it was just a matter of time before I would have to leave the country with my family and leave behind the deepest love I had ever known.

"Life goes on," the older women tell you when your heart is broken. And while that may be true, the heart does not mend properly. Part of it is always broken and always longing for the love that was lost.

Despite my broken heart, I had plans beyond marriage for myself. So, I swallowed my pain and made a decision: I would not marry Dhori at that time, because I needed to stay with my family and leave Albania. I was so deeply affected by my romance with Dhori that for many years I couldn't even say his name to myself. That handsome young man who was my first love passed away in Albania from prostate cancer on Valentine's Day, 2015. He left behind a wife and a son who had become a lawyer. I received the news of his passing from his sister, who had always wanted me to marry him. She told me that his family had loved me, which I knew and meant so much. Dhori had gone on to operate a thriving dental practice in Albania, ironically just like I did in the United States.

I reunited with Dhori only once, many years after my family's escape, when I returned to Albania for a visit in 1998. We had a chance to catch up and share the details of our families, but our lives had been lived separately. Once my family left Albania, my communication with him essentially ended since contact between Albanians and the outside world was forbidden by the repressive Hoxha government. I sent him postcards for a time, but when I learned that he had become engaged around 1968, the final blow was dealt to a relationship that couldn't be, and my fantasies about sharing a life with him came to an end.

Eventually, I was able to say his name again: Theodore, Dhori to his friends. In Greek, Theodore is translated to "Gift of God." We were Eni and Dhori, Dhori and Eni. He was my true gift from God in that because of him, I learned how deeply I could love.

10

OUR EXIT FROM ALBANIA

In 1966 my father started feeling increasingly nervous about remaining in Hoxha's Albania. I was 17 and in love with Dhori at the time, but I could see that the greatest priority to my father was to orchestrate my family's escape from the communist regime. But escape for my father came with a catch. He didn't just want to escape Albania for himself. He wanted the whole family to flee the repressive regime together. He worried that if I fell in love and got married, I would not want to leave the country. In his way of thinking, if one family member refused to leave, the whole family would have to stay, just to keep us all together – but remaining in Albania was not part of his plan. In addition to his strong desire to escape and live a life free from the constraints of communism, my father could see that this was the perfect time for our family to make such a move. All of his children were teenagers, with my older brother and I not long from embarking on the rest of our lives, but none of us had yet married. Dhori and I had moved on to a more serious stage in our relationship. My father could see that our feelings for each other might interfere with his goal of escape. I cared deeply about Dhori, and besides, how could I possibly go wrong in dating him? My beloved grandma had set up the relationship, after all.

About that same time, my older brother Elio graduated from high school. A math whiz, he desperately wanted to go to university, but the Albanian government, which ruled on such things, said he could not. Many things happened that way for my family since we were neither Albanian citizens nor Communist Party members. Elio did not want to give up his dream just because Enver Hoxha wouldn't allow it, however. Instead, he kept applying and jumping over every hurdle the government put in his way.

My father was a good man, but very stubborn. The critical issues facing our family were our lack of citizenship and his refusal to join the Communist Party. Ironically, the fact that we weren't citizens would turn out to be our path to escape. In the topsy-turvy world of Enver Hoxha's Albania, we were stateless people – though we were officially residents of Albania, we were neither citizens of Albania nor Greece. This type of predicament was common to Jews around the world at that time; and it left us all in the precarious position of not having any legal standing in the places where we lived, worked, owned property, and built our lives. In Albania, we were thought of as Greeks. Later, when we went to Greece, we were considered Albanians. My grandparents' and parents' old papers that proved we were actually from Ioannina could no longer be found by the Greek government. The documents would be "discovered" some 20 to 30 years later, but for now we were a stateless family, citizens of nowhere, with no actual legal rights or protections.

Our family's mixed use of language reflected our predicament. My siblings and I now spoke very poor Greek, even though we had spoken it quite well when we were young children. Greek had been our language in early childhood, but once we began to play with other children and attend school, we transitioned to Albanian as our main language. The Albanians around us thought we had an unusual accent. What we had was an Ioanninan accent, which was where my parents came from. They taught us Greek using their Ioanninan dialect.

My father's plan began with writing letters, and he enlisted me as his secretary. One day, he dictated to me a letter meant for the dictator, Hoxha, himself! In the letter, he stated that due to the laws barring foreign citizens like us from attending university, he was requesting permission for his children who were high school graduates to travel and study in Greece. After all, to the government we were Greek citizens living in Albania. We sent the letter. The mere fact that he dared to write directly to Hoxha represented an enormous risk for all of us. The communists had killed as many as 50,000 Albanians and erected reeducation camps for thousands more. My father could easily have been sent to one of those camps, or worse. Months passed, and then one day a government letter arrived stating that Elio had been accepted to attend university in Albania to become a construction engineer. In a way, my father's gambit had worked. Elio had been applying to university for a full year and now, finally, he could go. Shortly after that, a second government letter arrived which stated that I had been accepted to medical school. These were government-funded institutions, and we would not have to pay. Now my father saw that two of his children could potentially hold up his dream of getting us out of the country. While we were all elated over the educational opportunities, for the moment my father's plan for us to emigrate was put on hold.

But nothing proceeded smoothly in Albania in those terrible days. In this case, the Albanian secret police, the Sigurimi, found out about the university acceptance letters and were unhappy that the benefits of Albanian citizenship and membership in the Communist Party had been given to a foreign family that were neither Party members nor citizens. Members of the Sigurimi i Shtetit came to our home in their notorious dark suits and spoke with my father in our courtyard. They said to him, "Listen. Don't you think it's time now, since your kids are going to university ... don't you think it's time for you to become a citizen?" He thought fast and replied, "Of course I would love to be an Albanian citizen. We love this country. But there is family money back in Greece. If I become an Albanian citizen, I will lose my claim to it. Why should I leave all our inheritance to the Greeks?"

At the time, in the mid-1960s, tensions between Albania and Greece were high, as was resentment between the two nations, a fact that my father cleverly used to play his next card with the Sigurimi.

He told them that if he and his mother were granted permission to go to Greece and bring back our money, they would leave my mother and the four kids behind them in Vlora as security for their return. "Trust me," he said. "I'm coming back. I just want to go and get my money, bring it home with us, and we will become Albanian citizens." The proposition, which of course included the word "money," intrigued the skeptical officials. Before long, permission to travel, an extreme rarity in a country where few people held passports, was granted. It was time for my father and my grandmother to go to Greece. My father's plan was beginning to unfold.

In Athens, my grandmother's brother, Dr. Nisim Koen, was a respected surgeon who ran a busy private clinic – treating everyone from ordinary Greeks to high-government officials – with five floors of offices in the center of the city. On a warm, clear day in Athens, the family members met, embraced, and my dad made a request of his uncle. He said, "First, I would like you to give me a good checkup, because I never had one in Albania. Second, I would like you to help us get out of Albania. That's really why we're here."

My father's uncle agreed, and my father received his checkup and underwent X-rays, which revealed a cyst or tumor in his liver that was large, but fortunately benign and harmless. My father's uncle said that the tumor was something that did not need to be operated on, and that he could live with it for the rest of his life. My father's head was spinning. The tumor was exactly the excuse he needed for the next phase of his plan.

While they were in Athens, my dad and grandma also visited the office of HIAS, the Hebrew Immigrant Aid Society, an organization that had been helping Jews escape persecution in Russia and Eastern Europe since the 1880s, to get help with their own emigration. Next, since they had time, they flew to Israel to visit a great uncle from my father's side and other relatives they had not seen in many years. The trip could have been problematic for people who held neither visas nor passports, but when they presented themselves in Israel with the name Kohen, they were allowed to enter the country. At the airport, the Israeli immigration officials thought that my dad and grandma were just a couple of regular

Jewish immigrants. They confiscated some gold coins from my father, which he was not allowed to possess under Israeli law, but otherwise he and my grandmother were granted their visit (or so they thought).

After a few weeks in Israel, and a most pleasant visit with family they had not seen since 1938, it was time for Elia and Anetta to return to Greece and then Albania. It was then that they discovered the truth. Upon their arrival in Israel weeks earlier, and because of the language barrier, they had been incorrectly registered as Ole Hadash – new immigrants to Israel. They had been officially documented as such and were now subject to the Israeli government. This complicated everything because my father and grandmother hadn't intended to stay and immigrate, their plan had been only to visit relatives. Now that they were ready to depart, the Israeli immigration officials would not give them permission to leave the country. In a panic, my father told them that he and my grandmother had to return to Albania or the rest of his family who had stayed behind would be thrown in jail.

This was a real problem because my dad and grandma had no passports and no paperwork and were at the mercy of the Israelis. They had no choice but to return to the home of the relatives they had been visiting to ask for help and extend their stay while they figured out what to do. Luckily, those relatives had connections to the Mossad – the famed intelligence service – and after a few days my dad and grandma were allowed to leave the country and return to Athens. At the Athens airport, they were stopped by the Greek immigration officials and told they could not enter Greece because they didn't have visas or any proper paperwork. That's when my grandmother pulled a brilliant stunt: she immediately pretended to faint, and because she was such a good actress, the Greek officials transported her and my father to the hospital in an ambulance. Her brother, Dr. Nessim Koen, met them at the hospital and hustled back them to his place in Athens. Over the next few days, my father finalized the necessary travel documents for the whole Kohen family with HIAS, received his inheritance (about 5,000 lira in gold coins, enough to help him get started in the US), and headed back to

Albania with my grandmother. I do not know how my father managed to get those coins through customs, but he did.

That left open the matter of the money my dad promised to bring the Sigurimi i Shtetit from Greece. His permission to leave the country with my grandmother had hinged on this, as well as his promise to become an Albanian citizen. But upon their return to Vlora, my father suddenly appeared to be very ill. He moved with difficulty, seemed very weak, and looked quite frail. We were all so worried about him! When the Sigurimi i Shtetit came to our home, my father explained that he had taken ill in Athens and a doctor there had found a large mass in his liver. To prove it, he showed them the X-rays that had been taken by his uncle. Next, my father had us move a little couch to the front window in our house and he laid there all day so that anyone who walked by could see how sick he was. He soon told us the truth, but continued his beautiful act, especially when members of the Sigurimi i Shtetit would walk by and take a good, long look at him.

People would say to him, "How are you, Xhoni?" (That's what people called him in Vlora.) He would tell them, "Don't ask. I went to Greece and saw my uncle the doctor, and he told me that I am in bad shape and have to get an operation." Of course, none of this was true and he didn't need an operation at all. But he told the Sigurimi i Shtetit that he needed to go to Tirana to petition the medical commission about his condition, and they gave him permission to travel there from Vlora. In Tirana, my father went before a government panel of ten doctors who reviewed cases like his, to decide if permission to obtain surgery or treatment outside of Albania would be granted. Many communists at the time were sent overseas for surgeries that Albanian doctors were not equipped or trained to perform. If the panel determined that an individual needed such a special treatment or surgery, they would give approval for a medical trip.

In my dad's case, not one of the ten Albanian physicians was able to determine that his mass was benign and required no treatment, such was the pathetic state of Albanian medicine in the 1960s under communist rule. Because my dad was still a Greek citizen, permission was granted for him to travel back to Athens for the supposed surgery. His secret plan was now fully in motion.

Before that, however, the Sigurimi i Shtetit probed deeper, questioning him about the inheritance he had promised to repatriate from Greece. He told them, "To make a long story short, I didn't bring any money back because I couldn't sell our property in Greece." The truth was that there wasn't much property left in Ioannina after all, and what there was his sister had already sold to pay for the dye colors we used in our family's business. So, there was no actual money left to bring back. My father quickly changed the subject to his health and reminded the Sigurimi i Shtetit that the medical commission had agreed that he needed to travel to have the surgery abroad.

While this drama unfolded, HIAS in Athens continued its work of assembling passports and other documents for our family and finally alerted us that everything would soon be sent. We were finally going to leave Hoxha's Albania.

We began to pack in anticipation of our departure. On our street in Vlora, word passed freely from neighbor to neighbor about what was going on at our house, and there was no shortage of busybodies coming around to have a look. We were cleaning up the house and packing our belongings and the neighbors were asking us questions. After all, nobody in Albania was ever allowed to leave. People wanted to know who in our family would be leaving and we just told them that we would not know which of us would be accompanying my father until we got to the airport. I think that my father was trying to confuse everybody and let them think that not the whole family would be leaving, that some would stay behind. He was afraid that somebody might say something to the Sigurimi. He decided that the best thing to do was to say that we would all have to go to the airport to get our passports and that we wouldn't know until then. We told the neighbors that it might be just Abe going, or my other brother, Elio, or my grandmother, and it would be better if we just all said goodbye in case he died during the surgery. We had been renting our home, and we arranged for my aunt and her family to move into it after us. Eventually, we all went to the Hotel Viosa, in Tirana, to wait for our passports and to be near the airport.

We checked into a few rooms at the hotel and then waited, and waited, and waited. A full month went by without news regarding the passports, and we were running out of money. There was still some money in the bank in Vlora, but we wanted to leave it to my aunt, Zhuli Kohen, since her family was very poor and would be staying behind. Then one day, we received a strangely worded telegram. It came from Greece and was written in Hebrew mixed with Greek. It said that our passports were being held for us at the French embassy. At the time there were no political relations between Greece and Albania and so France represented Greece in such dealings. We should have been delighted, but something felt wrong. My father took my brother, Abe, with him to the busy French embassy building and they were able to push themselves in. He announced to the French officials that he was David Kohen. Immediately they told him that they had been looking for him for a month. They had seven *laissez-passers* ready for us. A laissez-passer is similar to a passport and can serve as a valid travel document. Later we found out that the Sigurimi i Shtetit knew all along that the documents had been delivered to the embassy, but never informed us. This incident was just one final indignity suffered by our departing family.

In many respects, I was a typical 17-year-old girl. I went along with most family decisions, though not all, and at that time I was not that interested in leaving Albania, mainly due to Dhori, which worried my father a great deal. The fact that we were supposed to close ranks behind the family patriarch when it came to major family matters led to a complicated and difficult situation for us all. My parents knew I was desperately in love with Dhori, and they didn't want me to run off with him. My father always said, "Either we all go, or no one goes." He had already insisted that we not leave Albania until Elio completed his studies in construction engineering, which he did. But now that Elio had his degree, it was time to go. To ensure that I wouldn't do something we would all regret, my parents locked me in my room at the hotel. I couldn't leave on my own until we were all ready to go. The room had a window, and I when I looked down, there was my Dhori walking back and forth, back and forth, on the street below. I could see him, but he couldn't see me. I was so young, and so afraid – I didn't know what to do. Finally, Dhori's sister came to the hotel and said to my dad, "My brother really loves Anna. He wants her to stay and says he would take good care of her. Why doesn't the family leave, but let Anna stay here?" My father told her that he would never leave his daughter behind; and with that, the romance of Anna and Dhori was over.

Soon after, on July 10, 1966, we boarded an Alitalia flight. We would fly to Rome and then Athens, as there were no flights from Tirana to Athens due to political differences between the two countries. We were accompanied by a plane full of Chinese passengers for the 90-minute flight—the Albanian dictatorship had close relations with China at the time. We were allowed to leave Albania carrying just one dollar per person. No meals were served since it was just a short flight, but the flight attendants did offer us bananas to eat. When we saw the bananas, we looked at each other and didn't know what to do. No one knew how to eat them since we had never seen whole, unpeeled bananas before (except in the Bollywood movies from India that for some reason were popular in Albania). We watched the Chinese passengers peel and eat them, and then we did the same and enjoyed them ourselves. We were so elated all through the flight!

Rome was a destination of choice and necessity for Jewish immigrants from Eastern Europe, something that continued through at least the 1990s. Once our family landed at Da Vinci Airport, we were met by HIAS representatives who had two large vans to hold our considerable amount of luggage. It was so nice to be treated with respect and assisted in such a time of transition. HIAS put us in a hotel in Rome, where we stayed for about three days. The Albanians hadn't allowed us to take cash out of the country, but we women were allowed gold jewelry, mostly bracelets and rings. Though we had gold, we still had only seven dollars between the seven members of our family – the meager amount the Hoxha regime had allowed us to leave with. This could easily have become a very dire and desperate situation, but my dad immediately sprang into action. He had cases of colorful Chinese parasols and cartons of Albanian cigarettes that we had packed and brought with us, and he went right down to the street and began selling them. Our family patriarch was a true salesman and always had an ace up his sleeve. After all, he had sold the feared Sigurimi i Shtetit on his surgery and talked his way into a new life in Western Europe for his family. In one day, he sold everything – all the parasols, all the cigarettes, and even some of our jewelry – and made $300. The real smokers in Rome loved Albanian cigarettes because they had no filters. At that time, $300 was a lot of money. Thanks to my father, we would not go hungry.

HIAS representatives, as well as those from the Jewish Agency in Europe known to many simply as Sohnut, checked in with us on our second day. While HIAS primarily settled immigrants in the United States, Sohnut worked to transition immigrants to a life in Israel. We told a woman from Sohnut that we would not go to Israel, but instead would go to Greece because that's where our extended family was. Then the HIAS representative arrived. She took one look at our young family and proclaimed that we were all great looking, *Che bella famiglia* ("What a beautiful family!") Then she said, "We're taking you to America." My father told her, "Oh no, we're going to Greece." Complicating matters slightly was the fact that there was an engagement party for my first cousin, Zakis David, set for a day or so later in Athens. We all hoped to attend, and we'd had clothes sewn for us especially for the occasion. The representative said to my father, "Well, if you don't want to go to America, then just sign these papers that say you don't want to go." My father signed the papers.

Our family had only those three days in Rome before we flew to Athens. We made it in time for the party, which was held at the exclusive Hotel Grande Bretagne, right on Constitution Square. The hotel was so spectacular, we all felt like we were in a movie. Here we were, finally free, reunited with our Greek relatives, and celebrating in style.

We moved into a house that my aunt, Nina David (the aunt I dreamed of when I was a little girl), owned in Athens and stayed there rent free until we were able to secure jobs. Before long, Nina's brother-in-law, Leon Batis, a Holocaust survivor, opened a store to sell fabrics. This was the break my father had been waiting for. His natural sales talents took over. After all, he had been a salesman in Albania as a younger man before becoming an accountant. In the fabric store, business picked up quickly and our family went to work. My father cut fabric and I helped. My sister got a job at a Marinopulos store, a well-known chain of pharmacies in Athens. My brother, Abe, started college, and my other brother, Elio, got a job as a construction engineer. Suddenly, we were all working and starting our new lives in Greece.

Yet the notion of a bright teenage girl like myself spending her days cutting fabric in a shop with her father was not what my parents had in mind for me. And to be honest, it wasn't what I wanted for myself. I had bigger plans and my parents could see that I was determined to get an education and seek out success in my life. My father said, "We must get Anna to school." He proceeded to pull some strings on my behalf through the Northern Epirus Organization – a Greek, government-backed, nonprofit organization that helped minority communities in northern Greece, and Greek minorities coming in from Albania, which had historically been Greece itself. This gave me a chance to better myself. I don't know how my father found out about this organization, but because of it I was able to get into dental school and resume my education – which in itself was a big accomplishment. Until then, I had been crying every day because I wanted to go back to Albania to my boyfriend. But when I got into school, I realized that at the very least I could finish my dental degree. I soon became happier, and my romantic wounds began to heal.

Before we left Albania, I had already completed two years of medical/dental school (medical and dental programs were taught concurrently in Albanian universities, requiring six years of education to become either a doctor or a dentist). In those days, becoming a dentist in Albania was considered preferable to becoming a physician, even though both were in short supply. Nevertheless, I decided after those two years to pursue the dental profession because, while we were still together, Dhori told me that if I became a doctor the communist government would send me to serve in a desperate village that may not even have electricity. That unappealing prospect was more than enough to guide my career decision, and fortunately in retrospect dentistry suited me well. When I restarted my education in Athens, school officials looked at my grades and told me that I had already done more than was necessary at that point. But, as I had attended school in Albania and not in Greece, they placed me in the third year of a six-year program.

Classes began in October of that year and things were looking up, until one day in the fabric shop my father turned to me and said, "Greece is not for us."

We had only been in Greece for six months, and although my father had done a lot to get Leon's fabric business going, it was not doing well, and Leon couldn't afford to pay my father much of a salary. At this point, we were not just poor, we were really poor. My father was frustrated in Greece and wanted another chance at a better life. We now had our citizenship, passports, and the freedom to live anywhere we wanted – my father didn't feel we should have to settle for living in a country where we would be poor. He wanted to go to the United States. I was exhausted at the thought of moving again to a new country. Besides, I was already in school.

Just as I had when we were leaving Albania, I protested. I said, "Pop, I'm not leaving. I'm not leaving again. I'm just starting school and I have to finish."

But my dad ignored my pleas and again visited the local HIAS office. He told them that we really didn't know what we were doing when we told their representative in Rome that we didn't want to go to America. He said that now we really did want to go to the US. Unbeknownst to my father, I met with Lydia Ashkenazi, another HIAS representative in Athens. I told her of my father's desire to emigrate to the US, but that I was concerned about where that would leave me in my pursuit of a professional degree. She explained to me that my best bet would be to finish dental school in Greece. She said if I left before finishing my degree, I would have to go through four years of undergraduate studies in the United States, and then start dental school all over again, which would waste a lot of time and money. This would turn out to be some of the best advice I'd ever received.

My father, however, had decided it really was time for our family to leave Greece and move to America, whether I joined them or not. While he hated the idea of me being separated from the family, he at least felt better about leaving me behind in Greece, which was a free country, as opposed to communist Albania. He understood how important it was for me to obtain my degree. So, his plans for the family move to the US went forward. In those days, the most common way to travel to America was by ship. Soon, in 1968, the Kohens, minus Abe and me, boarded a ship headed for New York. A year later, Abe sailed by himself to rejoin the family. After a weeks-long journey with almost nonstop seasickness, he called to tell me that when it was my turn to make my way to America, I should definitely fly!

Once in New York, the Greek-Jewish community helped my father and family settle into the Bensonhurst section of Brooklyn, where they were welcomed with love. They even found a few relatives who were living in the same area. With assistance from HIAS, they received some money for furniture. Ever resourceful and always thinking ahead, my father managed to carry with him from Europe the 5,000 Lira in gold coins from his inheritance, which he used as a down payment on a three-story Bensonhurst apartment building. He immediately moved the family into the upstairs unit and rented out the other two floors to pay the mortgage. In this way, the family was able to have a roof over their heads that was rent free. The Kohen family was off to a good start in America – thanks to all the scheming, acting, and trickery of my father. He had won! He had managed to outwit Enver Hoxha, his secret police, the medical commission, and everyone else who had tried to stand in his way.

11

SOCIAL LIFE IN ATHENS

Back in Greece, the house I had been living in with my family was now vacant except for me, and the landlord found a Russian immigrant family – the ethnically Greek Hatzopoulos family – to move in. They had a daughter, Lena, a bit younger than me, who was struggling and lonely in Athens because she spoke only Russian. They allowed me to rent a room from them because I spoke Russian and could be a help to Lena. There had been nothing good about growing up under Hoxha's regime in Albania, but he had required all children to learn Russian in school, which later would help my brother Abe find a job at a Russian library in New York and had served me well all through my life, especially now while living with a Russian-speaking family. So, I stayed there with the Hatzopouloses while I finished dental school. Our house was located at Promitheos 13, an address I'll never forget because it reminds me of the ancient Prometheus myth.

So, I remained in the house I had lived in with my family, which was close to my Aunt Nina – my father's sister – and the Hatzopouloses treated me very well. My social life, however, was missing a few things, most notably a boyfriend. It was 1966 and I was 20. It seemed as though everyone I knew was trying to fix me up. I went on dates, but I hadn't found anyone I really liked. In fact, shortly before my family left for the US, an older Jewish couple who were friends of my aunt's had come to our house for a visit and to make shidduch. They told my father they had what they said was "a wonderful man" for me – a young man with his own store and his own money. However, they wanted me to have a dowry. The man had his own fabrics business, so he really didn't need dowry money from this poor immigrant family who had left Albania with one dollar each to their names. In this meeting with the Jewish couple, my father had thought of his inheritance money (the money he would eventually use to buy the apartment house in Brooklyn) and said that he would be willing to give it up as a dowry for me.

From the next room, I could hear their conversation about this young man and the expected dowry. I was fuming. I opened the door to the room where my father was talking to the couple and I said to them in a loud, defiant voice, "I want you two out of here! I'm not blind and I'm not limping. I am perfect. I'm going to be a doctor very soon and I don't need your business guy to take my father's money. I don't want my father to give up the only money he has. I am not for sale!"

I knew the man they were trying to match me with, he was a nice guy, but he was not for me. Honestly, I was not ready to get married, so that was the end of that.

After rebelling against the Jews and the dowry system, and for the remainder of my time in Athens, I dated non-Jews. At one point I had a Greek boyfriend named Michael, whom I knew I would part with when I left the country. He wanted to marry me and took me to meet his parents. However, I wanted to finish school and make my way to my family in America. We also knew that as soon as he graduated, he would be enlisting in the Greek Army. I refused to marry him, or anyone, just because I might have been bored, lonely, or on my own. There was the possibility that Michael would join me in New York after his military service, which I thought that might work, so I hoped for that – but at the same time I knew that life might take a different turn.

During this time my brother, Abe, who by then had made his way to America and settled in New York, was going to City College for construction engineering and had found a job in a Russian library. He started sending me $25 each month to help pay my rent while I completed my studies in Athens. I had to live off what little remained. I was poor but I was happy. I really enjoyed spending time with the Hatzopouloses. We all spoke Russian, so we could interact easily, and we would sit and eat Greek food together. I felt like I had a family.

Then I had a brief but heartwarming visit to my true family in Brooklyn during my two months of summer vacation in 1968. While they had all gone to America by ship, I took my brother's advice and flew. My parents' apartment seemed so big to me, and we all had our own rooms, which was a real luxury compared to how we had lived in Europe. My parents seemed very busy, but also very happy. My mother was working in a cosmetics factory and my father was making food deliveries for a Greek restaurant – plus he was the landlord and owner of the building they all lived in. As always, my grandma took care of the home. My sister had a job as a keypunch operator in the computer industry. I met a lot of Greek Jews in the neighborhood, and we attended the Sephardic Temple. We had cousins I had not met before who had been in America since before the war, and it was so wonderful to connect with long-lost extended family.

I adored this chance to be a part of my family's new life in Bensonhurst, but I also spent some time exploring the city. On Delancey Street, on Manhattan's lower east side, I noticed a number of stores that were owned by Cohens. I spent a lot of time walking around and looking up at the tall skyscrapers. I had never seen anything like New York in my life. The city excited me, and I fell in love with it right away. I arrived speaking no English, but as I had an ear for languages and had already spoken three languages during the course of my life, I picked up some English during my visit.

Too soon, I returned to Athens, and that $25 from Abe did not go far. After rent, I had very little money left over. This made it hard to go out, spend time with friends, or to meet new people. Not surprisingly, near the end of each month there would be nothing in left in my pocket, no money even to eat. But my Aunt Nina came to the rescue. She knew I didn't have much food, so she made meals available to me whenever I needed them. I would go to her apartment and ring the bell, and when she buzzed to ask who it was, I would say, "Hi, it's lunch time."

Through the speaker I would hear, "Oh, it's lunch time again, is it? I bet you are hungry, Eni! Come on up. I've already put some food out for you."

My aunt was very sweet to me, and I don't know what I would have done without her. I was so broke during that period, that when the other dental students went out for coffee and food on our breaks, I would decline their invitations to join them and say that I was on a diet. I had no money for coffee, only enough for the bus.

My other aunt, the surgeon's wife, who was related to me by marriage, also treated me exceptionally well. Her name was also Nina, like my mother and my other aunt in Athens (so yes, two Aunt Ninas!), and she and her husband were part of a wealthy, aristocratic family. They showed me great affection and wonderful hospitality. In an important way, they served as role models. Once a week, Thia Nina would invite me to her house for lunch. She had a cook who made delicious Greek meals, and a maid who served us. I felt like royalty at her house, and she treated me like a princess. She was generous in other ways, too. At the beginning of every school year, she would take me to buy clothing and shoes and whatever school supplies or dental instruments I needed. She showed me so much love. She taught me what it was like to help other people. Because of her example, after I came to America, the only thing I wanted to do was to help others in the way that I had been helped.

I was moving along in my dental studies, and at this point when we did clinics we saw and treated real patients. We could invite people we knew to come and receive dental work from us, overseen by our professors, but it was hard for me to find patients this way because I didn't know many people in Athens. I found another way to see a good number of patients with a wide variety of dental needs, however. I knew that people who needed dental work often began to line up at the school as early as 7 a.m., so I would also arrive at that time and in a very official voice, tell everyone in line that I would be their dentist and to wait upstairs for me. This way, I took all the patients and got plenty of opportunity to hone my skills. The other students began to say that if "Kohen" was downstairs, there was no chance for anyone else to get patients. I guess I had a little more hustle than the other students, but they hadn't had to get in a bread line in the middle of the night to get food, like I did when I was younger. Getting to school by 7 a.m. and claiming most of the patients was nothing compared to that, and I wanted to get as much procedural experience as possible and be the best dentist I could be. I guess my motto was, "You snooze, you lose." As a result, my professors were amazed with my work, and I finished first in my class. All through my career, I attracted and kept patients through being personable, excellent at my work, and truly interested in their health and their lives.

12

COMING TO AMERICA

At last, I graduated from dental school, and I was ready to move to America for good. On December 23, 1970, the second day of Hanukkah, I boarded a flight to New York and was met at JFK airport on a chilly, rainy, but glorious evening by a representative from HIAS. She greeted me with a warm hug and my green card. At 24, it was time to start a new life and I could barely conceal my excitement. It was a perfect day indeed. I put my green card in my pocketbook and felt over the moon. The first time I stepped into America, I put on my Star of David necklace that I bought on a trip to Israel. It made me feel so good to wear it. I was happy and grateful to be Jewish in this wonderful country where I could wear my necklace without the fear of antisemitism.

I lived with my family and everyone was doing very well in America. Now it was time to look around and explore my new surroundings. My sister Alice took me to see the holiday lights in Manhattan, and I saw the angels at Rockefeller Center and the beautiful Christmas decorations. I kept staring at the lights, the people, the tall buildings, and I knew I was in a completely different and new world. It felt like I was dreaming, but it also felt so good. I was together again with my family. My father had finally accomplished his dream of having our whole family together, living in freedom. Here I was. I was in America. And not only that, I was in New York City!

I realized that the first thing I needed to do was learn to speak fluent English. My brother, Elio, was dating a Greek Jewish woman and in January they announced that they would marry the following winter. I became friends with my future sister-in-law, Telenia, and her sister, Lina, and we often accompanied each other on the hour-long subway ride from Brooklyn to Manhattan, where we were attending a language school to learn English. We practiced and shared our language skills each day as we rode the N train. One day, as we sat in the train, the subway crime that plagued New York in the early 1970s found its way to me. I can remember it so clearly. We were sitting on the train, talking as usual, when the train pulled into a station and the doors opened. In an instant, my pocketbook was gone. I jumped up and ran out of the train and onto the platform, followed by Telenia and Lina. The only thing I could think about was that my green card was in my pocketbook. I'd had my green card with me because in Greece we always kept our documents with us. It's a different world today, but back then I carried my green card because I didn't have any other ID.

We all left the subway, with me in tears. I tried to talk to the police, but my English was so poor, I could only manage a few words here and there. One policeman just shrugged and said to me, "Welcome to New York." To me, that was a terrible welcome. It took me six months to obtain another green card, which I needed not only for ID but to enable me to travel and reenter the country. Moreover, that green card represented proof that I was a US resident, if not yet a US citizen. I had no driver's license. Few Albanians ever owned cars or learned how to drive, so the opportunity had never come to me. By more contemporary standards, six months is not an extraordinarily long amount of time, but I was devastated to have lost my precious green card in such a way, and the wait for a new one seemed like a lifetime to me. But eventually a new green card (known less colloquially as a Permanent Resident Card), was back in my possession.

All the study and practice on the N train was beginning to pay off.

My English skills improved, and I felt like I could communicate with other New Yorkers and, most importantly, my future dental patients. So now it was time to take on New York City and look for a job. The *New York Times* classified section was the first place I looked. I, Anna Kohen, a dentist from Greece, was on the American job market.

My sister, Alice, told me to put on some makeup and wear nice clothes that made me look "dressed to kill." After all, she had been in the US for a few years by that time and had some experience looking for employment. I liked to work and wanted to get started, but there was just one problem: I had no idea how Americans got their jobs. *What do I do now?* I thought to myself I wanted to work in my chosen profession, but I had no contacts and no path to follow. No one I knew had anything to do with dentistry. But I wasn't about to let that deter me. I put on some makeup, a super-short miniskirt, a long coat, and a pair of knee-high boots (early 1970s "mid-winter" fashions) and took the train to Manhattan to find a job. I was 24 years old.

Soon enough, I was granted an interview with Dr. Leonard Linkow, a successful and – as it turned out – highly influential dentist with a posh 13th-floor office (13 happened to be my lucky number) at 30 Central Park South on the well-heeled Upper East Side of Manhattan overlooking Central Park. Dr. Linkow was a pioneer in the emerging field of oral implantology. He was the only dentist ever to be nominated for a Nobel Prize, which had occurred just a year or two earlier. Throughout his career, Dr. Linkow obtained 36 patents for devices and procedures in the field of dental science.

On the day of the interview, Dr. Linkow escorted me to his private office. I kept my Jewish star necklace very visible because my sister said from the name, it sounded like he was Jewish. I still didn't speak English very well, but managed to tell him that I was a good dentist from Greece who would like to work as his dental assistant, and I was a Jew, so could he please help me? He looked at me and said, "Okay, let me show you the office. Walk down this hallway." We proceeded to walk down the long corridor, with him following behind me. He showed me each exam room and hygiene bay. This would be my first job in the United States!

It took me a long time to realize why he made me walk down that long hallway after my interview. It was a little test that he had developed to see if a candidate was right for his office. If the interviewee walked slowly or quickly, Dr. Linkow would know what kind of employee they would be. I walked fast and he knew I would have the right energy for the office and help to keep his schedule moving throughout the day. And just like that I was hired! It sounds silly, but it's true.

I didn't know much English, but I proved that I could learn quickly as Dr. Linkow taught me the English names for each of the instruments. I knew well how to use them, I just needed to learn what to *call* them. It was a great place to begin a dental career. The problem was that I was hired as a dental assistant, not a dentist. But I quickly became the best dental assistant Dr. Linkow ever had. And little did I know, but my first boss in my first job in America was the pioneer of implant dentistry – a field he literally created by himself back in 1952. By 1971, dentists were traveling from all over the world to learn the procedure he developed, which decades later is still as revolutionary as it is effective. His procedures have given countless people back their smiles, pronunciation, and confidence – some for the first time in their lives. He treated thousands of patients along the way, personally placing more than 100,000 dental implants.

One day I made a suggestion that I thought could help increase the profits in his burgeoning business. It seemed that whenever colleagues in the dental profession would come to the office to learn the implant procedure, Dr. Linkow would not only teach them for free, but would also provide lunch, on the house. I suggested that the visiting dentists should pay for his knowledge, which they would go home and make money from, and they should also pay for the lunch he provided.

He said, "No Anna, I don't want to do that. I want them to learn. I want people from all over the world to learn how to do the implants." It was an altruistic offering, but as a pioneer in his field, Dr. Linkow was clearly shortchanging himself, and by extension, shortchanging his staff. But my boss was satisfied to make his groundbreaking procedures available to all who wanted to learn, and that was his choice.

My strong business sense came naturally – an influence of my father and grandmother – and it has served me well all my life. I've always had a drive to better myself. I would never be one to rest on my achievements, modest as they were back then. Because of this, I knew that I didn't want to be a dental assistant forever. I wanted to practice dentistry. The reality was that I would have to go through dental school again, and I decided it was time to begin. New York University offered an excellent three-year program, so I took out a loan and enrolled. School takes time, of course, and I approached my boss to ask if I could work half days. Classes ran from noon to 8:00 p.m., so he agreed to keep me on, working at his office in the mornings.

With my career in the US beginning to come into sight, I started looking at some other aspects of my life, too.

13

IN PURSUIT OF THE AMERICAN DREAM

Back when I departed Greece for New York, I left behind Michael, a dental student who was my somewhat steady boyfriend. The two of us attended school together in Athens, but when Michael finished the program, he was required to join the Greek army. We had discussed his post-enlistment plans, including the possibility that he would join me in New York. While I was never certain this would happen, I hoped for it, so I dated infrequently and remained loyal. When he finished his military commitment in 1971, Michael called me and said the words I'd been longing for, "Okay, it's time. I'm done with the army. So, what do you think? Are you ready to get married?"

I thought of a way to make this happen. I told Michael that I had been working in a great dental office in Manhattan, doing implants, while also nearing the completion of my dental degree at NYU. Things weren't just looking up for me in America, they were headed to the stars. I asked him to come to New York, learn about doing the implants, and then we could open our own implant clinic. At the time, implant techniques were still new to dentistry and my vision was that he and I would be among the first to offer the procedure in Greece, where I assumed he would eventually want us to live.

I paid for Michael's airline ticket, and he joined me in New York and stayed with us. The morning after he arrived, he made an unexpected proposition. He asked me to return to Greece with him, which wasn't a surprise. But he said we would stay with his parents in a small village on the Island of Lesbos. He had taken me there once before to meet his mother and father. But reversing course and returning to a village in Europe at this moment was not part of my plan. I had other ideas and told him flatly, "You actually want us to go to that small village and live with your parents? I can't do that. You'll learn the implants here and we will stay here in the US for a year and then go to Greece, but if not, we're breaking up."

I was still young, and I would have returned to Greece with Michael had he agreed to first spend a year in New York – and I would have married him even though he wasn't Jewish. But he didn't agree and the next day Michael boarded a flight back to Greece and flew out of my life forever. He was a young man from a small town, and he felt displaced in the big city. That chapter of my life, which had been lingering for so long, was now over.

So now it was finally time to socialize a bit more. I began to go out once in a while with my New York friends and over the course of these evenings met several Russian men, mostly in the Brighton Beach section of Brooklyn, but none were able to steal my heart. Later, some of those friends and I took a trip to Puerto Rico. We had fun and even went out to dinner with some other tourists, but nothing came of it.

And then there was Arturo from Mexico. Since I have not had contact with him for many years, I will withhold his name surname to protect his privacy. His mother and father were patients of mine in New York, and I became very friendly with them. They were wealthy Russian Jews living in Mexico City who also spent quite a bit of time in New York. They really liked me and invited me to visit them in Mexico City. I was flattered by their generous offer, and tempted to take a trip and see Mexico, but I was much too busy at that time. Arturo's father was a construction engineer and had built the Mexico City International Airport. They were well connected, rich and powerful. For a long time, I thought they were just interested in me as a Jewish person they knew in New York. Then one day, the wife had a gift for me, a gold pin, and she told me that she had a son. A son she wanted me to meet.

I was puzzled. They never told me they had a son. The next thing I knew, Arturo was visiting me at my office. Lo and behold, he was tall, dark, and handsome. We ended up in a restaurant in Manhattan; he asked to get to know me better and invited me to go to Mexico with him. I didn't hesitate before agreeing. Arturo arranged with friends at the Mexican embassy to speed up my travel paperwork.

I immediately went to Dr. Linkow. I said, "I am going to visit Mexico, give me a letter of recommendation in case I stay a few months and maybe I can work at a dental clinic." Linkow wrote me a letter that said, "Your gain is my loss." He was so very upset that I was leaving and all I could do was laugh. Sometimes I was sure he considered me his servant. He was often blunt and rude, and had truly begun to take me for granted.

Two days before I left for Mexico City, I was at a seminar with Dr. Linkow in Chicago and had arranged my flights so that I would leave from there. The day I was scheduled to leave, however, all flights were canceled because of a snowstorm. I arrived in Mexico City the next day, which happened to be Valentine's Day. Arturo greeted me at the airport with a lovely orchid corsage. He took me to his parents' beautiful house, replete with servants. I had my own room. I was amazed to see that everyone in the family had their own car. While I was there, Arturo bought his mother, a famous pianist, a brand-new light blue car. I lived with the family in Mexico City for three months.

Every morning Arturo and I went jogging in Chapultepec Park, the famous park in the center of the city that was the site of Aztec ruins. His family and I all lived as if we were on vacation for a few weeks, even though I was the only actual tourist among them. But eventually, they all resumed their daily lives and work – Arturo was also an engineer and worked with his father – and I had nothing to do. I registered with a Spanish language school where the students were mostly Americans. Within a couple weeks I was already conversational in Spanish, because of all the languages I had spoken throughout my life.

In his parents' home, Arturo and I had separate rooms across the hall from each other. Throughout my stay, I kept asking Arturo why he'd never gotten married. He was 37, attractive, and very wealthy. I could not figure out why he was still single. He answered that question with a wave of his hand, dismissing it. He simply didn't want to discuss it.

His parents were incredibly successful and well known. They took me to the President of Mexico's house for paella, and to other wealthy families' homes all over Mexico City – houses like I had never seen before, the richest Jews in Mexico City. But I didn't really feel any passion with Arturo. Occasionally, he would talk about a dear friend he had in a different city, a very special friend. I felt suspicious about this. While I was their guest, his mother constantly badgered me about how things were going between Arturo and me. In honesty, nothing was happening between us at all, and soon enough I decided it would be better if I went home. Arturo did not try to stop me. I felt certain at the time that after I left, he would soon be visiting his "friend."

Back in New York, an acquaintance of my sister's named Ruth had the idea of setting me up for a date with her boss – a tall, thin man named Markus De Rowe whose business was in the New York garment center. But he was divorced, and I refused to date a divorced man. I just didn't want to deal with their drama. I only wanted to date single men who had never been married, because divorced men had ex-wives and children and I didn't want that baggage in my relationship. I was totally against it. I was young, attractive, starting a career as a professional dentist and I knew I would not be alone for long. In fact, I had the pick of proposals from other New York dentists – many of them Jewish – who would regularly visit my office to learn the implant techniques. I stood my ground, kept my word, and only dated single men.

Meanwhile, Ruth gave my phone number to Markus and before long he called me at my family's home, announcing himself as my sister Alice's and Ruth's boss, and asked me out on a date. Because of my recent bad experience with Arturo, I tossed aside my preference for single men and agreed to see Markus, but for one drink and one drink only. I asked him to meet me the next day at the corner of 55th and Madison, near the gym where I often exercised after work. I told him I would be wearing white pants and that I had black curly hair.

The next day, after my workout, I went to the street corner where Markus had agreed to meet me. I approached a man who seemed like he was waiting for someone and indeed it turned out to be Markus, a stylish gentleman with European manners. He came prepared and hired a limousine to take us on our "one drink date."

Immediately, I was struck by his accent and asked him what his nationality was, guessing he was German. But he said that he was from Poland. I thought to myself, *Oh, he's European!* I did not want to marry an American man. I wanted to marry a European because I felt that we would somehow relate better to each other if we had similar backgrounds. Markus asked if he could take me with him to meet some friends at a restaurant. I agreed, but repeated, "Only one drink, right?"

We arrived at the restaurant, and I immediately felt uncomfortable. His friends were another couple who were hanging all over each other. In fact, everybody in that place was kissing and dancing in public. The scene was much too risqué for me. I didn't know Markus. I was suddenly very nervous that he would try to make a move on me too quickly. At the time, I considered myself conservative and square. Looking back, I can see that he probably just wanted to show me off to people he knew. My instincts told me that it was time to leave, but I still had not yet downed that one drink, my agreed-upon limit. So, I told him I did not like it there and proposed a change of venue. I suggested that we go to a place in Astoria, Queens, where a Greek singer would be performing. It was called the Zappion Pavilion. It wasn't a random choice. The Zappion, on Steinway Street, was at the time among the largest and best known Greek nightclubs in Astoria. It was a lively place, with bouzouki, drums, electric organ, and plenty of drinking and dancing.

The Zappion's singer, Vicky Moscholiou, was fantastic and I really wanted to see her. I figured this guy wanted to take me out and so I might as well take advantage of that. I thought, *Let's take the limo and see the Greek singer.*

But finding 31-01 Steinway Street in Astoria, in the famous

Greektown area, was more easily said than done, particularly at that time which was decades before the invention of GPS. The limo driver was neither amused at our search nor knowledgeable about Astoria and we drove around, seemingly in circles, as the night grew later and later. Markus kept saying that I was going to spend the night with him. I said, "Never." But he pointed out that it was already two o'clock in the morning, which it was.

Eventually, the driver found the club, but there were no seats available. Markus took charge. He found the owner and said to him, "Listen, I have this blind date here with me and I really like this girl. She asked me to bring her here. She's Greek, after all. So, what do you think? Can you do something?" He handed the owner a 100-dollar bill. The owner left for a minute then returned with a small, round table and two chairs from his office and put them directly in front of the stage. I was impressed.

We listened to the singer and her voice was beautiful. It felt good in the club, and in Markus' company, and both he and I knew that something special was happening. A peddler came in offering gardenias for sale, and Markus bought the entire basket for me, his blind date. But there was one problem: It was now at that point when it was both very late at night and very early in the morning. I had been calling my parents, who were still very protective of me, every hour to reassure them that I was fine and that I would be home soon. At about 4:00 a.m., Markus declared that he was hungry and had to eat. I rarely ate at such an hour, but Markus, this man from the fashion industry, insisted that we find some food. I reluctantly agreed and we took the limo to a breakfast spot in Brooklyn, not far from my family's place in Bensonhurst.

I arrived home at 6:00 a.m. When I stepped out of the limo, I took a glance upward to the third floor, and there were my parents in the window, watching and waiting as Markus and I said our goodbyes. We liked each other from the first moment. This was the first time I was ever late coming home. I told my mom that I was okay and that he seemed like a nice guy.

My father did not approve of my choice, at least initially. However, my grandmother was quickly won over by Markus. Two days after we met, he visited our house. Grandmother Anetta, hearing that my new boyfriend was there, immediately jumped out of bed – she was getting frail – and met him in the living room. No one in the house smoked, but there was Markus, taking deep drags on a cigarette in the apartment. My father was there as well. Then Markus declared that he was hungry, and calmly walked into the kitchen, opened the refrigerator, and began to rummage around like he had lived there all his life.

I was impressed by his casual way of making himself at home. I said to myself, *This is my guy.* I wanted him to be comfortable at my parents' house, which was nothing fancy schmancy. He was simple and easy like us and I liked that very much. Then my grandmother said to him, "Come here, sit next to me and give me a cigarette." She had never smoked in her life! So, the two of them were sitting there puffing away and she says, "I like him," in Greek: *Mou arései.* My father said, also in Greek, "I don't. He's divorced." Later, however, when my father developed cancer of the larynx, Markus became a favorite. He was the one who drove my father to his chemotherapy treatments and helped him in many ways.

From that time on, Markus and I saw each other after work nearly every night for two-and-a-half years. Still, I was taking the relationship slowly, primarily because I had violated my own dating code by seeing a divorced man, and one with two children at that. Plus, he was 11 years my senior, 40 years old to my 29. But those issues eventually faded, and we married in front of 150 friends and family, serenaded by an Israeli band and a Greek band at the palatial Terrace on the Park in the Corona section of Queens. Prior to the wedding, Markus had a plan. Realizing that he had no idea how to dance the *Zeibekiko,* the famous Greek wedding dance, without telling anyone he took lessons. When the music started and he began to dance, I thought, *When did he learn to do that?* Like our unlikely courtship, it was a wonderful surprise. I paid for half of the wedding myself, using money I had been saving to buy a red Corvette, a car I never purchased. It was a good trade. I got the wedding and the man. The car would have been gone in five years anyways.

Tragically, Grandma Anetta did not live to see the big wedding of her favorite granddaughter, her namesake, to this man she cared so much about. The woman who cooked, cleaned, taught, and in many ways raised me along with my siblings while our parents were out working, was gone. She was in her seventies when she died of breast cancer.

After the wedding, it was time for the honeymoon. We jumped on a flight to St. Martin, the charming French and Dutch island in the Caribbean. While there, we decided to take a boat to one of the small islands nearby. Our voyage started out great, and we even befriended a couple on the boat who were staying at our hotel, and we planned to meet them for dinner that evening. However, the excursion turned out to be a bad decision for me when I developed a terrible case of seasickness on the way to the island. Once we arrived, I told Markus that I was not going to go back to our island in that boat. Always the problem solver, Markus discovered that there was a small plane available that day to fly us back to our island. A very short flight, we planned to take the plane back and be rested and ready in time for dinner, which is what we did. But that night we waited and waited for our new friends, but they didn't arrive, and the evening was going by. *What happened?* we wondered with concern. *Where are they?*

When they finally got back to the hotel, they said, "You were the smart ones, taking that plane back. We had a terrible time getting here!" They explained that a storm had hit the area of that little island which kept them from returning in the boat until midnight. Markus and I had eaten dinner on our own but stayed up for drinks and to watch for our friends, who were so beleaguered when they finally arrived that they couldn't even think of eating. But they were also very happy and grateful just to be back on dry land!

In 1975, as newlyweds, we lived in a modest apartment on East 34th Street in Manhattan, a brief stroll from the NYU dental school on East 24th Street. My days began at 7:30 a.m. in Dr. Linkow's uptown office, and at noon I would hop on the subway and head downtown for my classes, which ended around 8:00 p.m. Then it was time to study, and very often I would not get home until 10:00 p.m. On top of this, I worked closely with Dr. Linkow in presenting his sought-after lectures and seminars, which dentists from across the city, across the country, and even from overseas, eagerly took in multiple times a week. It was a fast, ambitious, and seemingly endless pace that demanded a reservoir of perseverance, which I as a young dental student had in spades!

In October 1976, soon after I attended my last class at NYU and took my final exams, I accompanied the celebrated dentist on a trip to Munich, Germany, for an implant seminar. I prepared the instrument sterilization, among many other things. During the seminar, we wore these little hats to keep our hair out of the surgical field. It was Oktoberfest, and the night after our lecture we had a huge party. Of course, I took off my protective garment and my little surgical hat to attend the party. At the time I had long black hair. When I walked into the event, all the drunken dentists flocked to me – I couldn't figure out what was wrong with them. Finally, I realized what they were thinking: *Ah! so you were the one under that hat. Look at your long hair! You're beautiful!* I guess the combination of a young, attractive female assistant with cascading black hair who possessed prodigious knowledge about their profession generated a great deal of interest that evening among the mostly male crowd. They were harmless but enamored! I felt like a star in the making. Lucky for me I was not a big beer drinker, but that was a very fun, festive occasion that I really enjoyed.

When we got back to New York, I knew that my final exam results would be waiting in my mailbox. When I went out to get the mail, my hands were shaking. I opened the mailbox, took out the letter and saw my grades. "Oh my God," I screamed. "I passed! I passed! I passed!" I was screaming in the hallway. My doorman looked at me, asked what was wrong and I just yelled, "I passed!" I hugged him and cried because I was so happy. Then I went upstairs and called Markus, who was at work. I started calling everybody to tell them that I was a dentist now. It was such a happy day.

The next day, I told Dr. Linkow that I finally had my license and was now a dentist. By then, I had worked for him for five years as a dental assistant, at the highest pay level of a low pay scale. In other words, not for very much money. But now, at last, it was time for a change. A big change.

It was time to look for a new job.

At the time, two other dentists worked for Dr. Linkow. One was habitually late. I could not understand how a dentist with a regular schedule could come in late all the time. He left patients waiting and the staff didn't like it. I knew I could do a lot better than that. But with a full retinue of dentists on staff, albeit it one who strolled in on his own time, I had to search outside the Linkow practice to continue my career. The *New York Times* classified ads offered some hope. I began making phone calls and arranging interviews and spent hours on the subway, crisscrossing the city in search of my first job as a dentist. First, I went to Queens, then to a seedy area in Brooklyn, then back to Manhattan, repeating as necessary, but with no luck. I was suddenly facing a real obstacle to my dream of success – I could not find a job as a dentist! Undaunted, I knew I wouldn't give up. After all, I had faced adversity before. I had made it out of communist Albania, survived Greece with no money, and then thrived in America even when I was still learning English. Now, I had just won a hard-earned dental degree. I had never been the type of person to graciously accept defeat.

One day I called a specific office because I thought the location would be perfect for me. What happened? The hiring dentist said, "I'm very sorry. The position is filled." I wondered if he might have told me this because I was a woman. In the mid-1970s, the gender divide among dentists was wide. Males dominated the profession and female dentists were still a rarity. This was problematic for women looking to break into the field since it was a highly paid profession where women were not seen as being entitled to that sort of income. Even then, full-time general dentists earned well in excess of $100,000. Women back then did not make that kind of money, but the tide was beginning to change. The number of women students in American dental schools jumped by 20 percent between 1970 and 1980, and I found myself on the crest of that slowly building revolution. Even as recently as 2001, women comprised only about 16 percent of all US dentists, yet that ratio has risen in earnest in recent decades. According to figures from the American Dental Association, by 2018 out of nearly 200,000 working American dentists, 32.3 percent (or about 64,000), were female. A far cry from when I earned my degree in 1976 at NYU.

I began to understand the glass ceiling above me and felt myself staring down into the abyss of the gender gap as well. I had a sinking feeling that I wasn't finding a job because I was female. To test this theory, I asked Markus to call the number of the office that turned me down and see if they would give him an interview. He called as "Dr. Smith" and right away they scheduled an interview date with him. I was so upset. Back then I cried easily, and so I cried my eyes out. It was so unfair! I couldn't understand why this was happening. My patients loved me, and as a female I had a lighter hand when it came to treatment and surgery. I was especially talented at suturing. People were not used to having female dentists, and I understood that, but all I needed was a chance to prove everyone wrong and show them the excellence of my work.

Then one day, Dr. Linkow finally became fed up with his dentists coming in late. His father knew me well from my years working there and he told his son, "Lenny, why don't you hire Anna? She's the best thing you ever had in your practice."

But Dr. Linkow wasn't only my boss and a great dentist, he was also a male chauvinist. He didn't think his father should tell him who the patients loved. But he knew his father's words were true, and so did I.

Dr. Linkow reluctantly accepted his father's advice and decided to hire me. My career was finally about to get off the ground. I worked extremely hard at Dr. Linkow's practice. Besides having my own patient schedule, Dr. Linkow would often interrupt and ask me to give injections to his patients, who would request me because they knew how gently I could administer a shot. I would run back and forth between my patients and his. I worked so hard that I would go home and just collapse in exhaustion.

But I was so happy! I was finally immersed in the medical career I had dreamed about since I was a schoolgirl in Vlora. I was 31, a few years older than most new dentists but elated to be seeing patients and I truly loved my work. At the same time, my maternal clock was silently ticking, and I began to think seriously about starting a family.

Markus agreed and we decided we wanted to have two children. With that in mind we moved from our little apartment on East 34th Street in Manhattan to a larger high-rise apartment in Riverdale, a highly desirable section of the Bronx. Our life plan was coming together, and we were excited to start the next chapter.

Riverdale offered us an anchor, as well as an opportunity to educate our future children in a yeshiva, schooling that wasn't available to me in Albania. Our children would have Markus' Jewish education. Ultimately, we remained in our home in Riverdale for many years. It was a smart move made at the right time in our lives.

As if a rising career as a dentist in a busy, advanced practice on the Upper East Side wasn't enough, before my children came into the world, I decided to add even more to the already fast pace of my life. While I studied at NYU, the professors took note of the precise work I did. They told me that I was exceptionally good with my hands, better than most of the students and better even than some of my professors. Years before, teachers in Athens observed that same distinctive talent and ability. After I earned my license, officials at NYU offered me a position as assistant clinical professor of restorative dentistry. Thrilled and flattered, I quickly accepted the prestigious position and taught students there, in the hours after I completed my regular workday, for a full decade. My dedication to helping others trumped other considerations – including time commitments and traveling twice a week or more from lower-midtown Manhattan back to our home in Riverdale, where I would often arrive very late in the day. I have no regrets about the burdens it placed on me and Markus. After all, it was a great experience. I was able to help train Russian immigrants, since I was fluent in Russian from my time in Albania. I helped them pass their exams, gain the training they needed, and acclimate to America. It was a wonderful ten years, but that was enough. After I stepped down, I received a beautiful plaque of gratitude from NYU, of which I am very proud.

14

A NEW CHAPTER IN OUR LIVES

After we got married, Markus and I chose to delay having our first child to give me time to develop my dental career. By now I was performing dentistry in Dr. Linkow's practice, after working so hard and so long – across three countries, and in three languages – to become a dentist. Just shy of three years later I gave birth to a daughter, Felicia, and two years after that, a son, Olek. I worked throughout my pregnancies to the last day before giving birth, a practical choice since I was forced to use vacation time when the children were born because Dr. Linkow did not give me any time off at all.

I clearly remember the last days before I gave birth to Felicia. I was nine months pregnant, and it was a Friday, the day I always had my hair done. My official due date was just two days away. On the following day, Markus and I were watching TV when all of a sudden I heard "Boom!" and my water broke like a river all over the floor. We quickly cleaned up the mess with towels and then realized that because it was Saturday, Markus hadn't shaved like he did on weekday mornings.

"I have my bag ready," he said, panicking. "What do I do now?"

I took one look at him and said I wasn't going.

"What do you mean?" he asked.

"You must shave to say hello to your child," I replied.

Markus shook his head and said, "We're leaving."

"No," I said, "You had better go shave. I will not leave until you shave."

He got scared, hurried to the bathroom, shaved faster than he ever had before, and only then did I consent to leave for the hospital. Years later, Markus still insists it was ridiculous for him to have to shave that day. But I knew how I wanted him to look when our child first laid eyes on him, even though our daughter now says that her memory of that first meeting with her cleanly shaven father is somewhat fuzzy.

We made it to New York Hospital on East 68th Street in Manhattan with no trouble. Once there, however, nothing happened for what seemed like hours. Markus proceeded to wander off somewhere. Then the doctor disappeared, too! I started to have contractions. We had done our Lamaze classes, of course, and I planned to have a natural childbirth. The nurse went to search for the doctor. She found the two of them, Markus and my doctor, sitting next to each other totally asleep in the cafeteria. She clapped her hands and yelled at them, "Get up! She's giving birth!" And I did give birth to our beautiful Felicia, who graced her first minute in this world by going number two. The doctor just laughed and said, "You've got a healthy baby here!"

The next day, my parents arrived at the hospital. Our beautiful baby daughter was in the nursery of the maternity ward, and I was in my robe, looking through the glass at all the babies with Markus and my parents. My father said, "Who is it? Which one is it?" I pointed to Felicia and said, "That one. Pop, when she opens her eyes, she has these beautiful big eyes."

So, my father said, "Nurse, please. I go to Greece tomorrow. Please open baby's eyes." He didn't speak English too well. "I must see!"

"The baby's sleeping, Pop," I said. "We have to just let her be."

Eventually, Felicia woke up on her own and began looking around. She was so gorgeous, and we were all so happy. Pop and everyone who got to see those big, brown eyes was thrilled with our newest family member. Felicia was an extremely cute baby.

Two years later – while still working for Dr. Linkow – I again used vacation time to give birth because for the second time my boss refused to grant even the best dentist in his practice any paid time off. With a touch of bitterness, I accepted that my boss was stubborn and cheap. I worked every single day for him through the year, sick or not sick. Bad weather or good. I never missed a day's work through both pregnancies and worked right up to the last day of each one. After I gave birth and was quickly back at work, a few of my patients shared things like, "You know, Dr. Kohen, I just want to tell you that while you were pregnant and working on me, I felt the baby kick. It was so beautiful having a lady dentist work on me and get to listen and feel the baby's kicking."

Apparently, this baby boy, Olek, had spent a lot of his time in the womb kicking to let his mother know his wish, which was to enter the world ahead of his due date. This posed a bit of a complication for Markus, who was in Poland on business and not expecting me to go into labor while he was overseas. Without warning, I woke up early one Sunday morning with the sensation that water was dripping out of me – not the flood it had been with Felicia – like a steady, obvious dripping. I wasn't due for another three weeks, so I wondered how that could be? I got very nervous because Markus was away, and I was alone. I called the doctor and he told me to go to the hospital, check in, and he would meet me there.

I was suddenly hysterical. I needed to get to New York Hospital once again, but this time on my own. I waited until 8 a.m. so not to wake up my boss, Dr. Linkow, then called him. I told him that my water broke, and that Markus was out of the country. I asked Dr. Linkow to pick me up and take me to the hospital. He lived in New Jersey but said he would drive over right away. We had a live-in Polish nanny named Yadviga to watch Felicia.

When Dr. Linkow got to my place, he said, "Don't give birth now."

I said, "Don't worry. I'm not giving birth in a car."

I remember that he didn't seem nervous as he drove, but then he missed the exit for the hospital. I had to point that out to him, and he took the next exit and circled back through side streets. Finally, we arrived, and even though I was going to see my doctor, I was still three weeks early, not experiencing contractions, and I did not want Dr. Linkow to cancel any of my patients until I found out if I would have to spend more than one night in the hospital. I asked Dr. Linkow to please pick me up the next morning and told him I would come to work, which made him happy.

I was admitted to the hospital, and all seemed quiet until later that evening when my contractions began, and between 5 and 6 a.m. on Monday, March 24, 1980, I delivered baby Olek Asher De Rowe. Regrettably, Markus was still in Poland supervising factory production for the company he worked for, Christian Dior, but the baby and I were safe and healthy. I felt very strong and was fine. It didn't even occur to me that I should call anybody to come be with me.

The day Olek was born was a bit chaotic. Markus and I were living with Felicia in an apartment on the 27th floor in Century Tower, a high-rise on Netherland Avenue in Riverdale, New York. On ordinary days I would take a local car service to work, a schedule I kept five days a week. On that morning, there would be no work, but instead of simply focusing on myself and the baby, I called the limo service to cancel. I told the limo owner that I was very sorry, but that I could not make it that day because I had just given birth to a baby. The owner was astonished that I had bothered to call him. "Oh my God," he said. "You're so responsible!" Next, I called Dr. Linkow and told him I had given birth to Olek, and to cancel my patients. The office staff put together a large sign in the office that read: *It's a boy!* and hung it in the reception area.

Just a week later I began to feel the pull of my profession. My patients needed me.

Our housekeeper had been watching Felicia and continued to help me during my first days home from the hospital. Then Olek's bris had to be postponed after he developed a case of jaundice. On top of this, it was Erev Pesach, the day before Passover, and a Saturday. I thought, *Oh my God. We're not going to do the bris within the required seven days and Markus is so religious!* Markus had just returned from Europe. Things like this could cause me so much stress. But thankfully the doctor cleared Olek of jaundice at noon on Erev Pesach, and so the bris was done.

Other than family, just a few people attended the bris because of the holiday. That said, it all worked out, with a dose of irony thrown in. We found a good *mohel*. He did a perfect job and the boy who wanted to come into this world so early is now a grown man and exhausted from working hard and finding success. It is interesting, isn't it, how the wheel of life continues to spin, how I worked so hard once upon a time and now I watch my child do the same?

15

DR. LINKOW'S TROUBLES

Even the busiest dental professionals take time off on occasion and for Dr. Linkow, a vacation to Florida was finally squeezed into his busy scheduled. The Father of Implant Dentistry, as he came to be known, was also known for performing many operations each day with few breaks. Unfortunately, the stress of his work must have traveled with him. During the vacation, he suffered a heart attack, was hospitalized, and had open-heart surgery. Back in New York, I suddenly found myself in charge of his incredibly demanding practice. Overnight I took over supervision of 15 staff members, including dentists, hygienists, dental assistants, lab technicians and a young, attractive secretary, the same secretary, shall it be said, who was very close "friends" with the boss.

My added responsibilities further lengthened my workday and exhausted me. I even had to count the money at the end of the day to make sure all the numbers were correct. It was very tiring to say the least. Prior to Dr. Linkow's fateful trip to Florida, he and I had spoken about the possibility of bringing me in as a partner. I had raised the issue repeatedly with him over the years and was eager for an answer. But he had stubbornly refused to commit, even though a partnership with me would have benefitted him and his practice greatly. After all, I had grown very popular with the patients and word had spread, particularly among immigrant circles, which helped the practice flourish. All he would ever say to me was, "Well, we can speak about it later on." The clinical chauvinist was stifling his own practice.

Finally, Dr. Linkow returned to New York, fully recovered after his cardiac episode.

"Well, what about the partnership?" I asked him soon afterwards. He said I should speak to his accountant. With this flip answer I knew that he was saying no, once again. It was time to take matters into my own hands, and set the stage for a transition away from his office and his practice, so I replied, "Really? That's fine. And as of next week, you can tell your accountant that I am going to be working four days a week, not five." Linkow was stunned. I was much more determined and ambitious than he'd guessed I would be. I had firmly put my foot down, just like I had all those years ago in Vlora when I would hold my place in the ration line with a rock. Dr. Linkow did not fully understand all I had to do to survive while growing up, and he always underestimated me.

I'd had enough of Linkow's ungrateful stalling tactics. I went home that night, ate some dinner, and opened the *Times'* classifieds again, this time to rent an office where I could practice on my own one day a week. It wasn't long before I established my own practice at 130 East 63rd Street, in the Lenox Hill section of Manhattan, just off Lexington Avenue and less than a mile from Dr. Linkow's office. My office was small but beautiful. I hired an interior decorator who totally remodeled the space and made it modern and comfortable for my patients. My message to my boss and my reaction to his rejection were finally clear. It was now 1987 and I was beginning to transition out of his practice, which I did by 1989. All told, including my time as his dental assistant, I worked for Dr. Linkow for 13 years, my lucky number. It felt like I had done enough for him, even though he had given me my start.

It didn't take long to reap the rewards of my move. In that one day a week, spent in my own office, I made the same amount of money I was paid in an entire week working for Dr. Linkow. I could have left Dr. Linkow's office sooner, but I felt a debt to him for the great dental experience I had gained under him, experience that allowed me to have my own office and treat my own patients. I also felt a debt to the patients there. I don't think anybody in the dental profession has done as many full mouth reconstructions in their lifetimes as I did while working for Dr. Linkow.

Business at my private office took off. My rare and impressive dental skills, and the fact that I was a highly accomplished female with a light touch, along with my multilingual abilities – I could speak Russian, Albanian, Greek, and Polish, as well as English – set me apart from other practitioners and word spread quickly. It wasn't long before I added a second day, then a third, and eventually five full days to my schedule.

Word about my success soon spread to my mentor and part-time tormentor. Leonard Linkow, the Father of Dental Implants, finally announced to me that he at last wanted me as a full partner. But his leverage over me had changed, and this time I said no. He was too late. From now on, I would be a competitor, not a colleague. We did remain friends until his death in January 2017 at the age of 90. Not making me a partner was the biggest mistake of his life. He knew that and eventually told me so in my own office when he visited, not long after I opened it.

16

A RETURN TO ALBANIA

One morning soon after I opened my office, a new patient walked in. I told her that her name sounded Albanian, and she said, "Yeah, how did you know that?" I said, "Well, I'm from Albania," to which she replied in shock, "Oh my God!" What's more, this new patient worked right next door to my office. We started reminiscing all about Albania and she told me that every year, on November 28, the Albanian community in the tri-state area – thousands of people – celebrated Albanian Flag Day together. She also told me that there was an Albanian Mission nearby in Manhattan. I had absolutely no clue about those things. I had been so involved with my career, my kids, and my marriage, I'd had no time for anything else. I was also so busy with my new practice that I had never even thought of trying to find Albanian groups or resources in New York City. Plus, I didn't speak Albanian very well anymore because all my friends and family were Greek, and we spoke Greek together. I'd forgotten my Albanian since I had not used it for decades.

The next year, on November 28, 1988, I took a taxi to the Albanian Mission on East 79th Street in Manhattan to celebrate Flag Day with the expatriates. Since learning of its existence, I had gotten to know people at the mission, and they invited me as a special guest, which was such an honor. Someone asked me if I ever thought of going back to Albania and I said that of course I did, that it had been my dream for many years. My family and I hadn't really "escaped" like so many others who had risked their lives to leave the country, and we had not been politically involved in Albania since we left. We'd exited with legitimate documents and had never officially become Albanian citizens. And regardless of the reasons for leaving my home country, I'd long had a dream of returning. In fact, because Markus worked in the fashion industry and traveled often to Paris, I had applied several times over the years to the Albanian Embassy to travel back to Vlora, but I'd never received a response, official or otherwise. Ignoring an application like mine, I'd thought, was simply a typical Albanian-style reaction and I was far from surprised at the silence.

My New York friends at the mission, however, had big plans for me – their favorite dentist – plans that did not need the approval of callous embassy officials.

They told me that they would take care of everything and arrange travel not only for Markus and me, but also for our children to make the trip. Everybody would be able to visit Albania together! And because we would be traveling under the watchful eye of Albanian officials, we would not have to worry too much about the secret police and all the horrible things that still went on in the country.

I was speechless. What had led to this incredible opportunity? It had come courtesy of a senior Albanian government official who was grateful for something I had done for him. Shortly after I had been introduced to the staff at Albanian Mission, which was affiliated with the United Nations in New York, the country's UN ambassador visited my office suffering from a severe toothache. I treated him, and he thanked me warmly, but warned that if I charged him for the treatment, I would be taking the money from the people of Albania. Without hesitation, I replied that I'd had no plans to charge him anyway. As a matter of fact, I told him that I was planning to send a letter to the mission saying that I understood his position and that he didn't have insurance or earn a high salary since Albania was still under communist rule. For those reasons, I said it would be a pleasure to treat him and his staff free of charge for a year and take care of all their emergency needs including any necessary medications. This time it was the ambassador's turn to be astonished by a humanitarian gesture.

I asked the envoy whether I could bring a gift with me to Albania when I eventually went. He told me that I could bring along anything I wanted. He certainly could not have suspected that I had already come up with an ambitious plan. I told him that I was going to bring a new dental technique with me that was totally unknown in Albania. I explained that it was called the "bonding procedure," and I would bring the light machine and other specialized materials I would need. "The only thing you have arrange," I told him, "is for the university to bring me some patients." I would teach the professors how to perform this procedure and give them the equipment. The ambassador quickly agreed.

A few weeks later, Markus, Felicia, Olek, and I flew to Athens to obtain our visas ahead of our visit to my homeland. This gave us the opportunity to see some of my relatives who were still living there, even though our destination was Albania. When we reached the Albanian embassy, I was very pleasantly surprised to find that the wife of the Albanian ambassador to Greece happened to be one of my girlfriends from medical school! That chance encounter resulted in us receiving the royal treatment from Albanian officials. We also ran into my old friend, Dr. Zino Matathia, who had once been matched to marry me, and whose baby brother my mother had breastfed when his mother didn't have any milk. He was now a very famous doctor, and just happened to have been in Athens on vacation with his wife. We were, in fact, scheduled to fly to Ioannina on the same flight with them. Everything seemed to be going so smoothly. However, this luck did not last. Our flight from Ioannina to Tirana was canceled for lack of passengers. We had visas in hand – which had seemed like the hard part – but now, how could we get to Albania from Ioannina if there weren't going to be any flights? Eventually, my aunt called a friend in Ioannina to arrange for two taxis to accommodate our entourage and our extensive assortment of luggage, including dental equipment and all the many gifts I was bringing to my extended Jewish family. It was going to cost us a fortune to get us to the Albanian border by land, and we would be utterly cramped in the two cars. At the last minute we determined that it would cost the same to charter a bus and travel in comfort. It was 1989, not long before the fall of the Iron Curtain, and things were looking up in Eastern Europe, though communist rule was not yet over. I called Dr. Zino over – as he and his wife were also trying to find a way back to Albania – and invited them to travel with us from Ioannina to Albania. They could join us on the bus, and we would all travel to Albania together.

We traveled with 12 suitcases full of various gifts to give to our relatives, including clothing and custom-made jewelry that they would be able to sell. Then, in the middle of a hot summer day, our bus stopped at the Greek border because the Greek soldiers there would not let us through. The driver told us we would have to get out and walk the rest of the way to the Albanian border control, which was quite far away. I jumped up out of my seat. I hadn't come this far just to be stopped at the border! I ran over to the Greek border soldiers and I said, in Greek, that we were there from the US, and could our bus please take us to the Albanian side? Would they please not stop us? I added that it was really too hot to walk, and there were children among us, and we had so many suitcases to carry. Could they please just let the bus go through? One of the guards looked at me and said with scorn, "What would a beautiful lady like you do in a country like that?"

"Albania is my country," I said. "I was born and raised there. So, will you please let the bus go?" I explained that we were Greek citizens, that my father and mother were Greek, and that he should just let us go. And so, he did.

The bus moved slowly from the Greek border toward the Albanian border, bringing us face-to-face with the Albanian soldiers on the other side. Now I was suddenly nervous, all the fear I had lived under in my home country was coming to the surface. Speaking with the Albanian soldiers, I patiently explained that our flight had been canceled and the people from the government who had planned to pick up our group at the airport now had to pick us up at the border. It took a few hours for the government officials to arrive and in the meantime, the Albanian border soldiers decided they wanted to conduct a customs check on our 12 suitcases. They informed us that they were going to search them. I began to panic. If they opened the suitcases and found that everything inside was new – including jewelry and all kinds of new clothing that we planned to give to our relatives to sell and make money from – we would have to pay a huge duty tax for everything we were bringing into the country. We would not have packed so many new things if we had known we were going to enter Albania this way.

The situation demanded quick thinking, something I was good at. "If I were you," I told one of the suspicious soldiers, "I wouldn't open those suitcases." I explained that our people from the Albanian government were coming to pick us up, were in fact about to arrive, and that he should probably just wait for them. When they were here and could observe, I reasoned, he could open anything he wanted. Sure enough, the border soldiers began arguing among themselves, and of course they never opened the bags. They weren't customs officials in the first place, and of course they did not want to run afoul of the mysterious government officials we had on our side.

Soon, two of those officials arrived, and the situation was resolved immediately. Their two cars transported our family and our 12 suitcases, as well as Dr. Zino, his wife, and their bags that contained jewelry and some gifts for their family. Albanians then and now were extremely poor people and those who left always wanted to help those who stayed behind. Like me, he wanted to avoid paying the duty, so he threw his bags into the mix with ours. To tell you the truth, I was a little nervous because I did not know for certain what was in his bags, and I felt I could be putting myself at risk. But Dr. Zino described the contents in detail to me – just some simple gifts – which put me at ease to an extent.

Safely past the border and on our way, we were treated to a tour of southern Albania as our entourage followed the road toward Tirana, including Gjirokastër, the city where the dictator Hoxha was born. There, we checked into a hotel. The entire trip, including hotel and food, was free of charge as a thank you from the Albanian government, because of the dental services I had provided for the country's UN ambassador and his staff in New York. Being treated with such honor in Albania felt very surreal. After living there so many years under the repressive regime, I now realized how far I had come in my life. My family had left Albania years before in a manner so secretive, it had felt like an escape – each with one dollar to our name. Now I was an invited guest of the country, all courtesy of the same feared Albanian communist authorities that had kept our family waiting a month for travel documents that had already arrived. You had to be a communist to be an official guest of the country, but I that requirement was waived for me. I was considered a humanitarian who had helped the Albanian Mission in New York of my own free will. It had not been a fluke or a mistake. It had not been a random act of kindness by an Albanian sympathizer. The Sigurimi i Shtetit knew everything about me, and my family, and they chose to relent from their vicious, hardline policies in recognition of my work and what I had done for the country.

We soon arrived at the Hotel Dajti, a 1930s era structure near Rinia Park, on *Dëshmorët e Kombit* (National Martyrs) Boulevard in central Tirana. It was a sunny day, but our mood was even brighter. Everyone knew the Sigurimi i Shtetit were watching our every move and that the Dajti was bugged with microphones. After Dr. Zino handed me an envelope at the hotel that contained US dollars as repayment for money he had borrowed from me during our trip from Ioannina together, my old fears and paranoia that accompanied living in a totalitarian regime returned. The Sigurimi i Shtetit were everywhere, and I was really scared. I had not been back to Albania since leaving in 1966, but even now – more than 20 years later – the constant fear of being watched and the possibility of being arrested at any time that had been instilled in me during my youth was back in full force. In fact, this feeling has stayed with me throughout my life. I have been unable to shake free of it even decades later. But at the same time, I realized the significance of where I was and what I was doing, and because of this I managed to find calm on that first day in Tirana. I was back in my homeland and for once did not have to care about the Sigurimi. I was able to be simply happy. Relatives were dropping by and giving us a warm welcome. It was wonderful.

Markus was not left out of the activities. He was taken on a museum tour around Durrës and Tirana while our relatives watched our kids. But I had different plans. I was scheduled to be picked up the next morning by a professor and his chauffeur and driven to the dental school where I would begin my instruction for the other professors about the bonding procedure. There was important work to be done and the schedule was set, but then came an incredible twist: a car pulled up in front of the Dajti and the professor inside, the one taking me to the dental school for my demonstration, was my former boyfriend. It was Dhori! I was shocked! He was the same handsome man I had once loved, just older now. I didn't know what to do. I hugged him, of course, we kissed like friends, and he spoke Greek to me. He told me that he had been teaching at the university and I was happy to work with him since my Albanian language skills had drifted away after so many years. Clinical language would be an even bigger challenge. It was a long time since I had left him in Albania, and we had both had moved on and married other people. But for now, he would be my translator and we would work together. I never expected such a turn of events. There were other professors and people at the university who could have done the same job, but for reasons unknown he was the one chosen. I knew it was the Sigurimi i Shtetit behind it all, letting me know in a subtle way how much power they had in Albania, how much they knew about us all, even our most intimate secrets.

The seminars I gave were well received and greatly elevated the state of dentistry in the poor nation, making the long trip extremely worthwhile. I also donated VHS tapes to the university that described other cosmetic dental procedures. One of my friends there, Dr. Ruzhdie, was embarrassed to tell me that they didn't even have a television or VCR to play the tapes. I would eventually send them what they needed after I returned to New York, where I put an ad in the *Illyria* newspaper offering $50 cleanings with all proceeds going to the University of Tirana dental school. My hygienist would volunteer her services and we would spend a Saturday at the office playing Albanian music and cleaning teeth for this fundraiser. I would eventually write a check out to the university to buy televisions and VCRs, a check I handed to the Albanian ambassador to the UN personally. I have always enjoyed the pleasure of giving back.

There was yet another surprise in store for me in Tirana on that trip. One afternoon, a particular visitor came to see me at the university clinic, Inva Mula, the 21-year-old daughter of Avni and Nina Mula, both Albanian opera singers and composers. Years later, Inva became an international opera star in her own right, but for the moment she was simply a patient waiting to see me to have her teeth examined and worked on. At precisely the same time, I was scheduled to tour the Skanderbeg Museum in Krujë, one of the most visited museums in Albania. Plans aside, there was no way I would leave for the Skanderbeg without treating this young woman. As I was getting ready to leave for the museum, I saw her sitting there waiting for me to see her. She had tears in her beautiful blue eyes, and I decided I must see her before I left. After completing the young patient's treatment with the bonding technique, the budding opera star looked up at me and said, "I am 21 years old and never smiled. Thank you so much for giving me back my smile." It was more than enough payment for my work.

Over the next few days, we were given a tour around southern Albania, including another stop in Gjirokastër (a beautiful old Ottoman town and UNESCO World Heritage site), and a visit to the historic ruins in the ancient Greek and Roman city of Butrint, before settling into a different hotel, this time in my hometown of Vlora, close to the beach. At last, I was back home.

Relatives and friends visited us, and it was a great time for all of us. Markus found himself sharing his days with not just his wife and children, but with a steady stream of my relatives. At one point, he asked if we could have dinner alone. We went to local restaurant and the meal began intimately enough, but was interrupted after a cousin and four or five other family members joined in. It was all in a day's visit for us, we were so in demand on that trip! My husband could not understand why my relatives were coming to visit us exactly at dinnertime. But he was an American by that time and had lost the European sensibilities he must have had before he'd left as a young man. I said to him, "Did it ever occur to you that they wanted to be with us because I grew up with them, or maybe they were hungry because they don't have enough food, or any good food? So, whenever they visit us, it's okay. It's my family." Markus learned our Albanian ways quickly and before long he began inviting them to visit us himself, which led to more shared dinners, happy people all around, and an absolutely wonderful visit to Vlora.

It's not just sharing food that's an important social ritual for Albanians; we also love having a good time. One evening, some old girlfriends from high school including my beloved Cela and Eli visited me at our hotel. The hotel had a restaurant with a live orchestra, and to please us, the orchestra played songs from our teenage years in Vlora, a truly beautiful gift for us all. We danced and had a wonderful time, like we were those teenagers again. I finally felt like I had truly come home.

17

THE FORGOTTEN JEWS OF ALBANIA

Our 1989 visit to Albania could not have been more successful. And in many respects, the best was saved for the last. Before we left, I asked my old friend, Dr. Zino, for a list of the Jews still living in Albania, thinking that I could help them emigrate. For as much as I loved the country, since in 1966 when my family left, the government had become even more repressive – fully stamping out all religious practices, even going so far as to outlaw religious names for children. Dr. Zino gladly provided the list just before we returned to New York. Back in the city, I took the list to HIAS. I told the people at HIAS that we wanted to speak to them about the forgotten Jews of Albania, and that we still had family living there. I told them we had a lot of Jews on our list and that they were all Greek Jews. My first thought was to find a way to move everyone on the list to the US, but apparently only family reunions were possible through HIAS. The Jewish organization, Sohnut, would accept these Albanian Jews into Israel, but my goal was to bring them to America.

There was disappointment among the people who could not relocate to the US. Some were angry and even refused to speak with me after finding out they could only emigrate to Israel due to not having family already living in the States. I was also disappointed that we couldn't bring everyone to America. I carefully explained to them what had happened, things were smoothed over, and we remain friends to this day. I like to explain things and I am a natural-born problem solver. If my solution doesn't work, I don't get down on myself, I simply explain why it doesn't work and look for another solution if there is one to be had. Eventually, many of the people on the list were accepted to immigrate to Israel, thanks to Sohnut. At that time, there was no direct communication between the US and Albania, and almost no one in Albania had a phone anyway. Over and over, I called my older brother in Greece, who would call our relatives in Albania through a friend who worked for the Albania government and therefore had a phone. Again and again, I'd call to try and get messages to and from our relatives in Tirana. I spent a lot of time and money on those calls.

Next, I initiated discussions with HIAS regarding my family members on the list who were eligible to move to the US and made sure HIAS realized that it was important to get them out of the country. I wanted them to be safe ahead of the likelihood of political unrest in 1990. The Albanian government was as unstable as all the other Eastern European communist governments at that time, most of which would soon fall. I was worried that my family would get stuck in the country. Using the political situation as a pretext, I informed HIAS officials that my relatives' passports were due to expire on the last day of December that same year, to help them understand that the Jews who remained in Albania could be in danger.

My efforts finally succeeded. Two small planes were chartered by HIAS to fly from Rome – the center of Jewish immigration in Europe – to Tirana to pick up my family: 37 people in all. The first plane, which left on December 30, filled up quickly with about half the Jews on the list and immediately returned to Rome. The second plane was scheduled to arrive the next day, which was New Year's Eve and the last day that their passports would be valid, and those waiting for it in Albania suddenly became skittish and panicked that they would be left behind. It was terribly stressful for everyone, including me. But the worry ended when the second plane arrived and flew the remaining group to Rome, and life-changing safety, on December 31.

All 37 people, each of them relatives of mine, were flown by HIAS to Ladispoli, which once was a posh Italian resort community located approximately 45 kilometers (28.5 miles) northwest of Rome. It must have been a real culture shock to the new arrivals. Since the late 1980s, Ladispoli has served as a staging point for thousands of Soviet Jews seeking to immigrate to the US for resettlement. During that surge that occurred in 1989, more than 6,000 Jews arrived, which strained humanitarian resources in this town of just 17,000 people. At the time, it was said that Ladispoli was the only town in Italy where Russian was the main language – similar to the Brighton Beach section of Brooklyn, which is known to many people as Little Odessa.

The Shalom Club near Ladispoli's city hall was the main meeting place. According to a report published in 1989 in the *Los Angeles Times*, nationalist and neo-fascist Italians pushed back against the newcomers with antisemitic signs and graffiti. Despite all the turmoil, there were my 37 relatives with their eyes wide open, free of the oppressive Albanian regime, but in an unfamiliar country and hoping for their chance for a new start in the United States. Patience became a true virtue: it took six full months for authorities in Rome and the US to process their documents.

I was far from finished. Not long after my Albanian Jewish relatives arrived in Ladispoli, I reached out to the Sisterhood of Ioannina, a philanthropic organization of Romaniote Jews, and informed them that the 37 Albanian Jews in Ladispoli were of Ioanninan origin and needed help. I requested financial assistance in finding ten apartments for the refugees to settle in when they would finally arrive in the US. The Sisterhood of Ioannina ran an ad in their newsletter, asking for help, and the necessary money was quickly collected – enough to pay rent on ten apartments for two years. My parents, who were still living in Brooklyn, helped as well. The arriving Jews found work during their time in Ladispoli, and overall, these efforts allowed the ten families to settle in two-bedroom apartments in the Bensonhurst section of Brooklyn – living there rent free for two years thanks to the Sisterhood of Ioannina. It was hard to imagine a better start in their new country. They were blessed with a place to live, time to get on their feet, and had no need to borrow money to get by.

Back in New York, just as this was happening, I happened to have a Hassidic patient in my office and mentioned to him that ten Jewish refugee families were moving to apartments in Brooklyn and that I needed mattresses for them. "Let me make a phone call," he told me. A day later, a big truck pulled up in front of my parents' apartment building on 65th Street and 20th Avenue, loaded with mattresses. Each of the ten families received one queen- and two twin-size mattresses, free of charge. Things were going well and now, everyone had a place to sleep. I, too, slept better.

I still wasn't finished. Markus and I kept working to help the Jewish families get established. We placed an ad with the American Sephardic Federation and donations of necessities quickly began to flow in. We drove all over the city to pick up clothing that had been donated to "our" families.

I have to say that the resolve and organizational skills that I learned from my father and my grandmother made a huge difference in the lives of these 37 Albanian Jews, my beloved relatives, who emigrated with our help. They got a head start toward success in the US and I'm very proud of them. Today, one would never know that they were immigrants just 30 years ago and came here with almost nothing. We were able to provide them with a strong foundation of support and today they have beautiful lives, houses, and jobs. Some of them are dentists, some are doctors, and some are in finance. They have integrated extremely well into American life and are truly contributing to society. It's a wonderful story, and I'm grateful to have been a part of it. I'm very proud of them and love them all.

18

FINDING MY VOICE

Anyone who has had even a brief conversation with me since the late 1990s would instantly reach the conclusion, based on my raspy, gravelly voice, that I was either a heavy smoker or had yet to recover from throat injuries suffered in a debilitating automobile accident. Neither conclusion would be true.

I have never smoked and have always been a careful driver without an accident on my record. There is, however, an explanation for the rough sound of my voice that is in stark contrast to my demeanor. Rather than being caused by a sinister tobacco addiction, my vocal affliction is due mostly to stress.

Around 1994, Markus and I bought a co-op and moved to an apartment on 72nd Street on the Upper East Side of Manhattan, a big change from our home in Riverdale. Felicia and Olek were both high school age and had been accepted into a yeshiva in New Jersey. The school was known to be excellent, and we were proud that they would be going there, but transportation to and from the school presented a problem. The kids took a bus until Olek began to drive. Teenagers being the way they are, Felicia and Olek hated to get out of bed. I have always been punctual and found myself yelling at them every morning to get up. I raised my voice nearly every morning throughout their high school years, and eventually the strain took its toll. One morning, when Markus was in Albania on business, my voice finally succumbed to the daily strain. I recall that day clearly. I was by myself, working and taking care of the kids, when I started to feel that my voice was becoming a little hoarse. I didn't understand what exactly was happening. Right then, I came down with a very bad cold. I would usually take antibiotics if that happened since I was able to prescribe them to myself. And so, I self-diagnosed a case of laryngitis. I completed the full regimen of the antibiotics, yet nothing changed. I still felt ill, and the laryngitis persisted. My previous patients understood my condition, but new patients had to be told about my hoarse voice before they met me.

My father had suffered from laryngeal cancer and so I worried that the disease might have been passed to me, even though that form of cancer is associated with smoking and is generally not hereditary. My fears led to a procession of doctor visits. Acid reflux was believed to be a potential culprit, which led to prescriptions, including Prednisone. Still no improvement. Another physician advised me to initiate speech therapy.

A visit with a speech therapist uncovered an unexpected potential source of my affliction. Every time I met with this therapist, he tested my voice. One time he asked me to talk about my son. When I spoke about him, we both noticed that my voice was not too bad. Then he asked me to talk about Felicia. As soon as I mentioned her name, the machine he was using to monitor my speech registered a big difference. When I talked about my daughter it sounded like I had no voice at all. At the time, Markus and I were working through many of the typical challenges posed by a willful teenage daughter. But for a mother born and raised in communist Eastern Europe, I had deeply ingrained notions of child rearing and discipline, and my anxiety level over Felicia's headstrong behavior was very high. Living in Manhattan and having your teen daughter come home very late at night on weekends was stressful beyond belief for me.

A year of speech therapy passed with no noticeable improvement. Then in December, Markus' son Ari, known as "Alan" to family members, called from Israel to wish us a happy Hanukkah. His son, Ari, and his daughter, Deenah, had settled in Israel with Markus' ex-wife after their divorce, and Markus had been supportive of this because he was deeply religious and wanted his children to grow up there. Coincidentally, but also fortuitously, Alan was studying to become an otolaryngologist (ear, nose, throat, or ENT) specialist. I explained to him the obvious problem I was having with my voice. He said he hoped that I didn't have Spasmodic Dysphonia. No one ever mentioned such a possibility before. Spasmodic Dysphonia, a name which, ironically, is derived from Greek, is an extremely rare ailment caused by involuntary movements of one or more muscles of the larynx. Symptoms may include occasional or substantial difficulty speaking and one of several possible aggravating factors may be stress. Some doctors believe that SD, as it is known, may be caused by a virus, but that theory is unproven. I believed that Alan may have handed me an important clue, which was very exciting. He recommended that I see a neurologist (to perform and properly interpret the recommended neurological testing), who would then work with an otolaryngologist and a speech therapist to determine a proper diagnosis.

At one time, I told our family physician that whenever I felt stressed, I would lose my voice. Looking back, I was disappointed and angry that our family physician failed to look further into an appropriate diagnosis. Instead, he just believed what most lay people believed, that my condition was "psychological" and left it at that. As a dentist, I never hesitated to contact a specialist if I couldn't treat a patient on my own. My personal doctor failed me in that regard.

Once diagnosed, I gathered all the materials from the neurologist's office and took them to my doctor. I told him the news of my diagnosis tersely – in case he had another patient with similar symptoms that he might dismiss – and reprimanded him and strongly suggested that he read and learn from the materials I brought him. I then left his office, and never went back.

It took more than a year and visits to multiple doctors to find a correct diagnosis. I think I can be excused for harboring ill will toward the various physicians I saw during that time who were unable to diagnose me. Still, my reaction was not to scold, but to educate. I always treat people very nicely, and I also treat my enemies with love. Thanks in large part to my stepson, Alan, I finally had a diagnosis of this rare but truly upsetting disorder. In fact, I found out that SD afflicts an estimated 28,000 people in the US, a tiny number in terms of disease overall. So infrequently do physicians encounter a patient with Spasmodic Dysphonia that most have never even heard of it. Fortunately, there is a National Spasmodic Dysphonia Association dedicated to research and support for people who suffer from the disease.

Naturally, I refused to allow my condition to slow either my activism or my public-speaking efforts. I just don't know how to give up or quit. If I felt an audience couldn't hear me clearly enough, I would simply ask for the volume to be turned up on the microphone. My message always won out. Surprisingly, I struggled most not when addressing a large audience, but when speaking on the phone. For that reason, I asked friends and family not to ask about my voice, which would typically exacerbate the problem. Emails and text messages became a required substitute for telephone conversations. There is no cure for SD, although it has been found that Botox injections can have a positive effect. I began to schedule my appearances around my Botox treatments, which provided me with not just a measure of physical relief but also the confidence I needed to continue my speaking schedule.

That said, SD has not been easy to live or deal with. It's especially difficult here where I live in Sarasota, Florida, an affluent city which is home to many successful and accomplished retired people. Everyone loves the fine restaurants we have here, and simple pleasures like dining out become difficult for me if Markus and I are with people who don't hear well, of which there are many in Sarasota. If the people I am with can't hear me, I eventually become upset and frustrated. Sometimes, I just move closer to them and speak close to their ears. Even though I am by nature a positive, outgoing individual, my condition has caused me to withdraw somewhat from meaningful contact with others. Yet, I understand clearly that Spasmodic Dysphonia is not a death sentence. It's simply a part of my life. The only thing I can say is that it could have been worse. I have a condition that cannot be treated, but thank God I am otherwise healthy. If this had started at the beginning of my career, it would have been devastating. But I came down with it after age 50, and thankfully I was already established and confident in my abilities.

The search for cures and treatments for orphan diseases like SD, illnesses that affect relatively small numbers of people, generally make it unprofitable for drug and medical device companies to pursue remedies, so relief from SD has been stymied by lack of research. Because of that, unlike the situation concerning far more widespread diseases like heart disease, cancer and Alzheimer's, the SD community is in the position of having to continuously seek financial support to aid sufferers. While attending a support group of people with SD, I offered to raise money by cleaning their teeth at a reasonable price and donating the money to the national association. It was a small, but meaningful gesture since it emanated directly from SD patients themselves. Since then, I have done this and donated the funds to SD for several years.

There may never be a cure for Spasmodic Dysphonia, but even if there is, one thing is certain: I will never allow the disease to get in my way. In the meantime, I regularly travel to Miami for my Botox injections, which provide at least temporary relief.

19

THE SINGING DENTIST

There is a time in every person's life when one looks back and reevaluates their personal goals and expectations. For me, first and foremost, the lessons in kindness I learned early on have led me to live a life of helping others. I believe the decisions I have made along the way reflect that. Since I was a very little girl, I wanted to be a doctor, because I wanted to help people and make them feel better. That idea never went away. It's part of my blood. I got the idea from my grandmother and now I think my granddaughter has gotten it from me.

I attained my goal many times over. But healing work was not the only notion I have held since childhood. Many years ago, I also wanted to become an entertainer. I sang in the kitchen while washing dishes when I was young, and I thought I had a very good voice. In Vlora in the warm months when we opened our kitchen window, I loved to do the dishes and sing my lungs out. I had such a voice that people passing by would stop to listen. They could hear me, but they couldn't see me. I could see them, though, and once I saw that people were listening, it made me want to show off even more. When Markus and I would go with friends to Astoria, Queens for a night out at our favorite Greek taverna, I would always get up and sing with the singer. Everybody there called me *The Singing Dentist*. The best times were when I sang just for me, even though I had fun singing with my brother, who even got me to stand up and sing one night in a Greek restaurant in New York. So, I kept singing. I guess I got that from my mother's side because everybody on her side, including my mom, had a beautiful voice. The day, years later I found that I could not sing anymore, I was devastated.

Spasmodic Dysphonia robbed me of the pleasure of using my lyrical voice to sing in front of others. The condition not only destroyed my musical dreams, but it made a struggle of simply talking. I had become a blind painter, a deaf musician. There would be no more singing Greek and Albanian love songs, no more operettas for me. Music and songs had been such an important part of my life. I felt tremendous sadness, knowing I would never again sing the way I had before. These days, I sing by closing my eyes and hearing my inner voice the way that it used to be.

20

FAMILY HEIRLOOMS

In 1989 when Markus, our children, and I visited Albania and Vlora, we were fortunate enough to pay a visit to the humble street where I grew up. We even stopped by my childhood home in the Jewish section of town. My old home was now a rental unit, but we were allowed inside where we saw my old bedroom (now just a storage room), and the fireplace where my family and I made coffee in the early mornings and where my grandmother cooked all day. It was at that fireplace, when I was 11 years old, that I was badly burned after I tried to use gasoline to light the fire and it blew up in my face. Grandma Anetta, ever smart, quick thinking, and resourceful, sent someone to the village to get a lamb, slaughter it, and return with the fat from the animal, which she then applied to my wounds before I was rushed on foot to a nearby hospital for treatment.

I thought back to the day of the accident, still so clear in my mind. When I burned my face, my grandmother did everything in her power to get me the help I needed as quickly as possible. I recovered and healed very nicely thanks to her careful and attentive efforts, and without any burn marks on my face. I have never felt self-conscious, and no one would ever guess that something so devastating happened to me. My grandmother and I had such a deep connection – we loved each other so very much. In those moments after the explosion, she knew just what to do to treat my burns and preserve my looks, and I am forever grateful to her for that. In her later life, when she was living in New York, she gave me some jewelry, true keepsakes. Among the pieces was a pair of gold and ruby earrings that are believed to possibly be 250 years old. Their fine craftsmanship is so apparent when you look at the plain little loops. Every time I wear them, I think of my grandmother. I treasure those earrings dearly.

I also think of my own granddaughter, Alana – Felicia's daughter and only child – when I wear my grandmother's earrings. When I see my beautiful Alana, I see a copy of myself with the same cascading head of curls. The only difference is her sparkling blue eyes. Alana has blue eyes because she got her grandfather's genes from Poland. I tell my darling little Alana that I am her Nona, and that I also was a little girl once with a Nona. I tell her that my Nona loved me very much and that she gave me a pair of earrings, and that one day when Alana grows up, she will have those earrings. Alana gets very excited when I tell her that those beautiful earrings will be hers one day.

21

VERY ALBANIAN AND VERY JEWISH

Most people are placed into simple categories, either by themselves or others, and one of the principle categories is one's nationality. In that regard, I have now become fully American. But people have asked me over the years what I consider to be my own identity. After all, I was born in Albania to a Greek Jewish family and my heritage is neither simple nor typical; it's very unusual. I tell anyone who asks that I am an Albanian Greek Jew. That I am both very Albanian and very Jewish.

In June 1967, after the Six-Day War, Israeli tourism was in shambles. To help the tourism industry – and perhaps to attract new, young immigrants – Jewish organizations in many European countries began sponsoring free trips to Israel. So, in July of that year, my three siblings and I traveled from Athens to Israel with about 30 other young Greek Jews. My father gave each of us $50 to spend during our two-month trip. The Jewish organization sponsoring our trip took us by bus all around Israel. Since it was right after the war, we saw many Arab-captured towns and cities and were able to see a large part of Israel in a very short time.

As it was the middle of the summer, the weather of course was very hot. We were constantly thirsty and made a lot of stops to buy water. My ability to speak Russian helped because many of the shops we went into were run by Russian Jews. They appreciated that I could ask in Russian for cold water, which they gave us right away. Actually, the first words we learned in Hebrew were *majim karim* (cold water).

In exchange for our free trip, we also had to volunteer to work on a kibbutz, a communal Israeli farm, of which there were hundreds in the country. We stayed on a kibbutz for two weeks, waking up each day at 4:00 a.m. and picking pears until 7:00 a.m. We were shocked to discover that there were many non-Jewish people from Europe who had come to Israel to volunteer on the kibbutzim. We had only been living in Greece for one year at that point and we couldn't understand why people from other countries would come to help Israel. We were very impressed with that. Of the many Jews from other countries who we met, we related best to the Italian Jews, probably because we had often heard Italian music on the radio back home in Albania. While on the kibbutz, every afternoon we learned traditional Israeli folk dances. I loved having this time to travel and learn so much about Israel and its culture.

The kibbutz experience was unbelievable, and my siblings and I had the best time ever. After our early morning work in the fields, we would go to a communal dining room for a huge breakfast of boiled eggs with lots of fresh vegetables like tomatoes, cucumbers, and scallions. After that, we'd tour the country in kibbutz vans, and learn about and enjoy the sights. But the greatest part of all was meeting our Uncle Isaak, our Aunt Betty, and our first cousins Matti and Malka in Tel Aviv. My uncle and my mother had not seen each other for many years. During World War II, my mother married my father and moved with him to Albania from Ioannina. Around this same time, my uncle moved to Athens. The rest of the family who had remained in Ioannina were deported and murdered at Auschwitz.

While in Athens, Uncle Isaak worked for a Greek man who decided to help my uncle escape when he heard that a ship was leaving that day from the Port of Piraeus. The ship was heading to what was then Palestine, is now Israel. My uncle hurried to the port, but when he arrived, the ship had already left. He was told that there would be another the next morning, so he waited for that departure. While he was waiting, he learned that the ship he missed the day before had been bombed by the English, killing everyone aboard. With a heavy heart for those who were lost, he took the second boat and ended up in Palestine, where he settled. He didn't know the whereabouts of anyone in his family and thought everyone was dead. A few years later, he met my grandfather's brother, Joseph, who lived in Ramat Gan. Joseph told him that my mother, Isaak's sister, was alive and well, married to Joseph's nephew, and living in Albania. So, my mother and uncle were the only members of their Ioannina family to survive the Holocaust.

When my mother found out that her brother was in Israel, she was overjoyed that she might get to see him. At the time of our visit, few people had US dollars, and everyone wanted them because they held their value while all our currencies fluctuated. Everyone who could afford to bought dollars on the black market. We had a few dollars with us from my father and we gave them to my uncle to sell for us on the Israeli black market, which gave us a bit more spending money for the trip. Communication with my uncle and his family was very difficult and complicated. He spoke Greek, but my aunt was Turkish. She did know some Greek, but we mostly used our hands and communicated creatively during our visit. Meanwhile, our cousin Matti spoke a little Greek. Our cousin Malka, however, didn't speak a word of Greek, so she tried to speak with us through Matti. In any case, we loved meeting our cousins and our uncle and aunt. Uncle Isaak, a very funny guy who was a great dancer, loved Greek dancing and Greek music – we enjoyed plenty of this during our time with them. The whole trip to Israel was wonderful, a very special time for us all.

Though I was still a student, I told the people in the kibbutz that once I finished dental school I would like to return and work there for a month or two for free. I now had two loves, Albania and Israel. I would do anything for those two countries. I've been doing a lot for Albania ever since, but not as much as I should have for Israel. I focused on Albania because it was a newly freed society lacking in direction. Albania had so little and needed so much help and I was very happy to share my experience and knowledge with the Albanian community. Israel already had connections and was much more established, but I keep a special place in my heart for this wonderful country.

At one time, in fact, a friend and I set out to volunteer for the Israeli Army, only to be told we were not needed. My willingness to help Israel always existed. Yet, my deep pride in Albania persists. Most people know about Albanians like Mother Teresa and perhaps Ismail Kadare – the famous novelist, poet, essayist, and playwright. They are from an earlier generation of Albanians. More recently, notable Albanians include operatic soprano stars like Ermonela Jaho and my old friend Inva Mula – and that's just to name two. The moment the borders opened in 1991, so many talented Albanian young people finally had their opportunity to shine. Now, they travel and live outside Albania and have become rather well known.

Following the death of Hoxha and the end of communism, educational opportunities underwent remarkable changes. Albanian students were previously confined to attending universities in the Soviet Union and studied using almost exclusively Russian language textbooks, but the fall of the Iron Curtain gave them a chance to take advantage of educational opportunities in the US. Many were suddenly able to attend Harvard, Columbia, NYU, and other prestigious schools in the West.

I learned from Russian textbooks throughout my education in Albania and was able to speak and understand the language. My first two years in medical school, in fact, were spent learning from books and classes in Russian. But the many intervening years eroded my Russian considerably and, because of that, my ability to speak Russian well has fallen away.

Albanians in the 21st century have migrated around the world. Many live in urban centers in New York, Detroit, Tampa and elsewhere. And many are beginning to use their newfound freedoms and abilities to attain wealth, especially in the West, and to donate funds to help those still in the old country. While hospitality has always played a large part in Albanian culture, monetary donations are by and large not part of the Albanian ethos. But many are learning the importance of contributing financially and have started to help in critical ways. At least some of their initial reluctance can be traced to the long, hard years under communist rule when few outside the Party had any money at all and fewer still understood the principle of borrowing money in order to succeed in business and build the economy.

In Albania, as in other Eastern Bloc countries, citizens were kept literally in the dark about the Western world. I grew up that way and those who didn't experience that kind of life firsthand have difficulty fathoming the difference between the way we lived, and the way people lived in Berlin, Paris, London, or New York. When I was young, Albanians didn't have televisions, refrigerators, vacuum cleaners, or almost any other modern conveniences. If you never left your country, then you can't know what you're missing out on. If you can't watch TV, you don't know what's going on in the world. But we did have the "Forbidden Books," as we would call them. We also called them the "yellow books," because they were so old. We kept them hidden and passed them to one another in great secrecy. These were mainly great works of literature like Tolstoy and Dostoyevsky. We appreciated these literary masterpieces as much as those who could freely read them in other countries, maybe more so, and we protected our forbidden copies and kept them circulating for as long as possible.

Although there were no televisions in Albania, there were radios to listen to even though they were banned. Our family had a radio, and we were obliged to use it only in secret. I loved listening to the Festival of San Remo from Italy, a singing competition like today's Eurovision. I knew every word of every singer of my generation. Radio was our favorite form of entertainment.

In January 1998, my older brother Elio came to visit the family in Brooklyn. It was a very cold winter that year. He came because my father was not doing well, and he wanted to see him before he died. Coming from Greece, Elio was not dressed properly for the cold and became very sick. He was the only one of us who liked to drink and smoke, and when he went to hospital, he was diagnosed with not just a cold, but a heart condition. The recommendation was that he should have immediate open-heart surgery.

During Elio's visit, on February 28, 1998, my father passed away after suffering from heart problems and dementia. We begged our brother to stay with us after our father passed and stressed that he should have his heart surgery in the US. Even though he was a trained construction engineer, remaining in Greece as his wife had wanted meant he hadn't been able to use his degree. Instead, the couple owned a boutique, which he ran. They also had two daughters, Ninette and Malkita. Despite our pleas, my brother returned to Greece, due to his many responsibilities. There, his condition worsened, and he was admitted to the hospital. He had open-heart surgery but did not wake up after the operation. This was all too much to take for my mother, to lose her husband and possibly also her oldest child in quick succession. My mother, sister, and I flew to Greece. Elio was in a coma and on a ventilator when we got there. The doctors had waited for us to arrive before taking Elio off life-support. He died before our eyes on April 14, 1998, at age 54. Alice, Abe, and I were heartbroken to lose our eldest sibling, and so soon after losing our father – and our mother was absolutely devastated. Both of his daughters would go on to marry Greek Jews, with Ninette marrying the famous graphic designer, Viktor Koen, from Thessaloniki, settling in New York, and having two children, Sivan and Elio (named after his grandfather). My brother's younger daughter, Malkita, also married a Jewish man from Thessaloniki and they have three children. My brother would have loved to see his beautiful grandchildren.

We sat shiva for Elio in Athens, along with my mother, who was staying with my brother Abe. He had married a very beautiful Greek-Jewish girl named Seli Yohana, and they had two daughters, Fidji and Graciella. Fidji would eventually marry a man named Robert Chimera and have two children, while Graciella enjoyed remaining single. After we sat shiva, it was time to return to New York. At the international departure terminal at the airport, I handed over my US passport. The official looked at my passport for a very long time, much too long, then called over another official. I knew that many Albanians had been using phony documents to escape the country, and I guessed these officials were suspicious of me since it said that I had been born in Albania. But my brother had just died, and I grew very impatient and outraged at this scrutiny and delay. I threw my credit cards and business cards at them to prove I was an American and doctor of dentistry. I shouted, "Shame on you for treating me this way just because I was born in Albania! Our brother has died. We just want to go home. Why are you doing this to us?" That was enough and they let us through. We cried the whole way.

After we got home, my mother decided she could not live alone at her age and moved in with my sister Alice. Alice had gotten married before me, to a man named Joseph Masri, a Jew from Alexandria, Egypt. They were religious and had five kids, and eventually, 18 grandkids.

Even though she had never smoked, in August 2003 my mother died at age 83 after suffering for two years with lung cancer. She was a great, strong lady who always had a smile on her face. I took Fridays off the whole time that she was sick, so I could accompany her for her chemo treatments. Every week I brought flowers to the facility to give to the other patients to help them feel at ease.

One of the last Fridays that I took care of my mother, she sat in a chair while I changed the sheets on her bed. She was totally exhausted. She touched my head and was mumbling something in Greek while I sang old Greek songs to her that I knew she liked. Eventually I could make out what she was saying: "May God bless you."

The next morning, my sister went to check on her and found her taking her last breathes. She passed a few minutes later. It is very hard to lose your parents. I miss mine every single day.

22

A DENTAL FEMINIST

Women's issues and women's rights have always been important to me. In Albania, particularly during my early years, women were treated as slaves by their families. There was no gender equality, even under an allegedly egalitarian communist regime. When a girl or woman got married in Albania, it was assumed the bride and her husband would live with her new in-laws. Every time someone came to visit, the bride had to go to the kitchen, make coffee, and serve everyone as they sat around talking. Even the mother and the grandmother would expect to be served. I saw that with my own mother, living under my grandmother and grandfather's roof. My mother had no power. She was like all other women in Albania. She went to work while our grandmother did everything at home. And even when she came home, my mother would be subservient to my grandmother, who continued to rule the roost. Years later, all of that changed and today women in Albania are allowed to work. Some have become professionals. Dentistry, I think, is the best profession for women because they can open their practices inside their homes, which is very common in Albania and Greece. That said, women in those countries are still responsible for child rearing, cooking, and housekeeping, which they must make time for, often between seeing patients. So, things still aren't equal. The men, of course, have the same jobs outside the home they have always had. My own knowledge and experience with those disparities has shaped my views throughout my lifetime.

After I saw up close how women were treated in Europe, upon arrival in the US, I was already a strong women's advocate. I found myself naturally drawn to the growing women's liberation movement, which stood for equal rights, equal opportunities, and equal personal freedoms for women. My attraction to the movement was also born out of my own experience with the glass ceiling, when in 1976 I recruited Markus to test the willingness of a dentist to hire a woman. When Markus pretended to be a dentist looking for a practice to work in, he got more calls for interviews than I did as a fully degreed and licensed woman dentist. That experience hurt me so much. To me, it highlighted the need to stand up for women, particularly women in dentistry, who were a distinct minority at the time. I knew I had to do something. I believed so much in women's progress. I wanted women to be equal to men, and sometimes even better than men. A female dentist has a lighter hand when it comes to surgery and is more sympathetic toward her patients' pain. It took many years of struggle to make a difference, but we were the ones – the tiny percentage of women dentists in the 1970s and 1980s – who fought for females in dentistry to have equal opportunities in the profession. Today, women dentists are very common, a fact I'm very proud of.

As the heated politics of the 1970s feminist movement roiled American culture, not to mention how it changed the job market, I shied away from overt political activity. Being a New Yorker, I was keenly aware of movement luminaries of the day like Bella Abzug, Gloria Steinem, Shirley Chisholm, Betty Friedan, and my friend Ruth Messinger. But my frenzied schedule allowed me little free time, and I was only able to support them from afar.

Through it all, I still worked to continue my father's legacy, a legacy that I am happy to be known for: helping Albanian Jews leave Albania.

It is also through that unique lens that I view the contemporary struggles of people who immigrate, whether from Albania or any other nation. As a Jew in 1971, it was easy for me to come to the States, immigration was totally different at that time. My parents applied for me as I finished dental school in Greece. I was able to come to America right through the airport and had a Green Card waiting for me. Today, immigration is completely different. I do believe that there should be a priority to keep families together when it comes to immigration. If sometimes there's a husband and a child in one country while the wife and mother remain in another country, that family should definitely be brought together. The laws in the 21st century are so different than they were in the 1970s, but there is also so much change in the world in general. There are wars that create enormous numbers of immigrants, who are really refugees, and they go from country to country trying to find a safe place to live their lives in peace.

I think of the story of the infamous MS St. Louis, a German ocean liner that carried more than 900 Jewish refugees from Nazi Germany who sought to escape antisemitic persecution in 1939. In similar fashion to the Syrian and North African refugees some 80 years later, the Jews of the St. Louis were repeatedly denied permission to land by both the United States and Canada. The ship ultimately returned to Europe where some passengers were resettled in the United Kingdom, Belgium, and France. But many others were turned away at every port, and ultimately given up to the Nazis and murdered. We need new laws on immigration to make the process fair. People are being persecuted because of restrictive immigration and emigration laws currently in force around the world.

More specifically, I have continued to assist women, particularly Albanian women, in vital areas such as healthcare. I work with Albanian women to try and develop programs to help them because they come from a country where they don't have proper medical facilities and don't have knowledge about things like gynecological exams, birth control, or breast cancer awareness. Of course, they need to know that they should go to the dentist, too!

I have also worked alongside the American-Italian Cancer Foundation, which has offered free mammography screenings in a room in the Bronx House, a large New York neighborhood center with strong connections to the Jewish community. The idea was to encourage all women, particularly poor women with no health insurance, to undergo the life-saving exam. In addition, I have worked to help women select an appropriate educational path and develop job-finding skills – assistance that is particularly critical for newly arrived immigrant women with limited education and minimal English-language skills. These women are also often fearful of a healthcare system they do not understand. I am concerned for women in the Albanian and other immigrant communities who are desperately seeking ways to establish themselves in their new countries.

I have devoted my life to promoting, supporting, and participating in humanitarian activities, including serving as president of the Albanian American Women's Organization. During my tenure with this incredible organization, we partnered with the Rotary Club of the Bronx and Gift of Life International to send nearly 20 children from Albania to Italy for life-saving heart surgery. I've been honored to work with organizations such as the AAWO, and to help the people of Albania – especially the children – in every way that I can.

23

MOTRAT QIRIAZI

Founded in 1993 by Shqipe Biba, and incorporated by myself in 1999, the Albanian American Women's Organization – *Motrat Qiriazi* (in short, the AAWO, or Sisters Qiriazi) is a nonpartisan, membership organization based in New York City. It serves as an educational, advocacy, and support group and is the only group in the US that addresses the needs of Albanian women and girls. The AAWO's mission is to empower Albanian American women and girls to achieve their full potential by providing them access to a range of resources, emotional support, guidance, and information. AAWO aims to lift the status and spirit of the Albanian American community by promoting the integration of Albanian Americans into the social, emotional, and cultural life of the United States. In addition, AAWO works to strengthen the bonds between Albanian American women and their sisters all over the world. Motrat Qiriazi is named after the sisters Qiriazi, the first Albanian women educators who, in the early 20th century, opened the first school for girls in Albania.

Over the years, the organization fell into a degree of inactivity and its programs suffered as a result. On occasion, I would attend an AAWO event in New York, ask whether they needed additional funds, and then write a check in support of their activities, much of it to help the children of Kosovo.

One day in November 1988, prior to the beginning of the bloody Kosovo War, a woman from the group called to invite me to a meeting in Manhattan. I remember it was a Monday. She said, "Dr. Kohen, we are having a board meeting. Would you like to join us?" I asked, "When?" and she said, "Today."

I went and it was nice. They talked in general about the organization and its future and mentioned that they needed a new leader. I chimed in and pointed out a few women who I thought could do the job. It never occurred to me that what they had in mind was to choose me as their president. But before I knew it, they nominated me, and I was humbled when the vote was unanimous. So, there I was, a Jewish girl as their new leader, ready to take on the responsibility and help the organization get back on its feet. I like to laugh about that because as a Jew and part of the "chosen people," I had finally become an actual "chosen one" myself. Albania shared a close connection with Kosovo as most Kosovars are ethnically Albanian. Because the Albanians saved the Jews during the Holocaust, they looked to us now to help save them from the Serbs in Kosovo. Many Albanians in New York at that time were cleaning and maintenance workers. They asked the Jews who lived in the buildings they worked in for donations. I think being Jewish was at least part of the reason I was chosen by this amazing group of people to serve and guide their organization.

Rather active in many New York circles that could benefit their mission, I set about networking and putting the right heads together. I was ready, willing, and able to provide a much-needed jumpstart to a program that had been lacking in leadership and energy and be able to garner the financial support necessary for the group to address its mission successfully. I was enormously flattered and surprised, but also unaware of exactly what I was getting myself involved in. Sensing my concern, Markus asked me that night whether I was certain that I should take on such a critical, but time-consuming position. I was determined and told him, "If I can help the community, I'll do it."

What the community truly wanted was a woman in charge who could rebuild the group. I started quickly by applying for non-profit status. Next, with 501(c)(3) status in hand, I renamed the group the Albanian American Women's Organization – Motrat Qiriazi, a more recognizable name and a far easier sell for a group based in the United States. I established its headquarters at my office address in Manhattan. The AAWO was officially certified in October 1991, and we were primed and ready to push ahead with our initiatives.

In the Balkans, the situation was quickly deteriorating because of the civil war. I took a call from the Vatra (translated as "Hearth") – a venerable political organization based in the Bronx – in which they asked me to join them in New York for a meeting with Chuck Schumer, then a US-Congressman representing parts of Manhattan and the Bronx. They asked me to tell the Congressman my personal story, as well as the story of how Albanians saved many Jews in my country during World War II, and that there was no reason why our brothers and sisters in Kosovo, which was 90 percent Albanian, should suffer this terrible genocide.

The people from Vatra warned me that Schumer had a reputation as a talker, not a listener, but this did not throw me. It was my chance to step up. At the meeting, I immediately launched into my speech. I wouldn't let him stop me. I explained that Albanians saved Jews and that NATO had to get involved and do something, which is exactly what happened. Schumer took note and listened carefully. The effort to urge NATO to intervene later moved to Washington. President Clinton ultimately did intervene, a decision that forever made him a hero in Albania.

That winter, January 1990, I got another chance to help my new cause, this time in Washington, D.C., where I was invited to speak alongside Representative Tom Lantos of California, a Hungarian-born Jew and Holocaust survivor. My choice of topic was "Never Again." I prepared the speech without realizing that the audience was mostly made up of Jews, and since the event was held on Capitol Hill, people came with signs, many of which said, "Never Again," which made me feel good and made the speech even better. The event gave me confidence in my efforts as a leader, and the AAWO picked up steam. Not long after that event, I spoke before another large crowd on the steps of the Capitol where we raised nearly half a million dollars. I had no experience working with a nonprofit, but I was making a major difference for an organization that had once teetered on the edge of extinction. Under my leadership, the AAWO quickly became not just solvent, but able to use its resources to funnel aid to people in Kosovo during the war.

Next, I was recruited for a board position, this time with the American Jewish Joint Distribution Committee, also known as the Joint or the JDC, a large and very respected group that had been helping Jews since World War I. It wasn't long before still others took notice of my work, and we began to receive checks in the mail from across the US. What began with moving my relatives out of Albania to the US expanded to helping many others back in Europe. The AAWO took in $144,000 during this period as people rushed to help. I also managed to raise an additional $30,000 and distribute it to three outside nonprofit groups, one in Tirana and two in Kosovo, and I am ever grateful for their help. I instructed the secretary of my dental practice to personally send thank you notes to each donor. My staff was always eager and happy to help with these things as they also believed in the importance of doing this work.

When the war in Kosovo started in early 1998, refugees began to flee the conflict and streamed into the US. In response, the AAWO applied for funding from the federal government through the Office of Refugee Resettlement, the ORR, which is part of the Department of Health and Human Services. The AAWO was the only women's group to apply. Because I was not versed in the inherent red tape and pitfalls of this complex type of government funding, I hired a consultant who agreed to work pro bono until funding was secured. In addition, since the AAWO office was, in fact, the office of my dental practice, the work and the endless line of people looking for assistance became a distraction that was impossible to keep up with. Soon, Albanian women were coming to the office asking to see Motrat Qiriazi – the actual sisters themselves. They didn't understand that was only the organization's name, and actually thought they were going to find the Qiriazi sisters in my office. Regardless we were happy to help them as we could.

One day, I took a call from an official in Washington at the ORR. Funding totaling $1 million had been granted to us to be used over a four-year period. It was truly stunning news. With that, I immediately opened – with the help of Delina Fico – the first AAWO office, which alleviated the crush of people flooding my dental practice. Ms. Fico was brought in to work at least temporarily in the Manhattan office and a small staff was hired – including Shqipe Malushi, a writer and human rights activist from Peja in Kosovo, to be executive director. The organization was growing quickly and along with that growth, its ability to help in a war-torn region was mounting. People would come and knock on our door, crying and scared, and we had women there ready to help. We did everything we could for those refugee women.

To bring in the most assistance possible, I often turned to the connections I had acquired through my social circles and also through my dental practice. For example, one of my patients was the owner of a toy company and I persuaded him to provide toys for refugee children living in Boston, where thousands of refugee families had settled.

Meanwhile, refugees from Kosovo were fleeing to nearby Albania to escape the war and the brutal ethnic cleansing campaigns of the Serbs. The numbers were staggering. According to a report published in May 1999 by *Migration News,* by the end of April 1999, about 600,000 residents of Kosovo had become refugees and another 400,000 were displaced inside Kosovo – meaning that half of the two million residents of Kosovo had become refugees or internally displaced people. About 375,000 Kosovars fled south to neighboring Albania and 150,000 moved to Macedonia. Still others moved to Montenegro, to Bosnia, and even as far away as Israel, which went a step further by sending doctors to assist. Tent cities were set up in Albania, but many other people were accepted by Albanian families, even though few of those families could afford the burden of helping others. Yet, they took these refugees into their homes. Once I learned about the humanitarian crisis, I quickly decided to help, and I sent Shqipe Malushi to Tirana to observe. After her report back to me about the situation, I made an executive decision that our organization would send $500 to every Albanian family who was housing a Kosovar family, an enormous amount of money in a country where per capita income was a little over $100.

Eventually, Israel took in hundreds of Albanian refugees from Kosovo and placed them in kids' summer camp dormitories. Tents were set up to serve as temporary medical clinics for these refugees. Among the physicians who treated the Albanians in the Israeli camp were Dr. Zino and a Dr. Balaj, a high school classmate of mine. I happened to be on vacation in Israel with Markus at that time. I went to the camp and gave a speech to the refugees about the AAWO and asked how we could help them. I was so impressed with what I saw there. The refugees were being treated well and their children were playing and happy. Many of them were learning Hebrew and about Israeli culture.

With demand soaring, we added three more AAWO offices on the same floor where we were located in the New Yorker Hotel. We now had 12 full-time staff. The AAWO newsletter continued through community support. Funding was steady from 2001 through 2005 when, as the war drew to a close and interest among donors waned, financial support began to taper off. By 2005, funding had been reduced to a trickle and I decided to give up most of the office space, lay off paid staff and run the once-large operation solely through volunteers. The contraction of office and staff didn't matter too much to me because we were able to get funding to help the refugees during the peak of the crisis. We were there for all the women who needed us and even helped them with resumes and in learning English.

As outside sources dried up, the AAWO turned to the local community for help. People would joke that when I had a patient in the chair, I would tell them, "Hey, listen, I need money for the organization. Can you promise to give me a check because otherwise,

I'll pull your teeth out." But I always asked nicely and my reputation as a passionate fundraiser on behalf of the Albanian community preceded me. When the AAWO celebrated its 25th anniversary, I was presented with a Lifetime Achievement Award in New York. I am so very proud of the work I did for them. Making a difference through that organization meant a great deal to me indeed.

I was now starting to think about retirement. Markus and I had long talked about moving to Florida for our golden years, and I especially wanted to find a beach area that would remind me of the beautiful beaches that rest on the Adriatic in Albania. It was clear that with retirement and a move to Florida, my interests and commitments would have to be scaled back, even if my passion for life had not ebbed. One of the first major commitments I had to let go of was my board presidency with the cherished AAWO, the group I had poured so much energy into for so many years. I stepped down from that position in 2016 after working with the remaining board members to hand off the job to the vice president, a woman I had mentored for years, and someone I hand selected as my eventual successor. The name of this remarkable woman is Beti Beno, Esq.

But that did not mean I had broken away completely from the group. I founded a Florida chapter of the AAWO from my adopted home of Sarasota.

Then in 2017, I began organizational work on yet another large event. A year prior, Markus had introduced me to Orna Nissan, who was working at the time as program director for the Jewish Federation of Sarasota-Manatee. My first question to her concerned International Holocaust Remembrance Day, which was coming up the next January 27th. The question drew nothing but a blank stare. Not only was no event planned to recognize this important day, but Orna was completely unaware of the occasion. It didn't take a minute to offer myself as a volunteer along with my willingness to attend a meeting to plan a commemorative event at the Jewish Federation. With that, I became the founder and chair of the local International Holocaust Remembrance Day annual event.

My thought was to begin the commemorations by spreading awareness that Albania had saved many Jews during the Holocaust, and I began by discussing my ideas with leaders of the Albanian community in Tampa Bay and Clearwater as there were very few Albanian Americans in the Sarasota area. I spoke with presidents of the two most prominent Albanian organizations: Vatra (the Pan-Albanian Federation of America), and the Albanian Heritage Foundation of Tampa Bay. I did not want to hold this event alone, so I put these two wonderful organizations together with my organization, the AAWO Florida Chapter. I aimed to hold the event in Sarasota. In effect, I set myself up to plan the entire thing! But such preparation came as second nature to me.

It turned out that the head of the Heritage Foundation, Dr. Ardian Kraja, was a DJ as well as a doctor. I quickly seized on his musical expertise and connections, recruiting him to provide entertainment for the event (pro bono of course) and requesting that he bring an Albanian dance group from Clearwater. After all, it never hurts to ask!

Next, I invited the Albanian ambassador to the US, Floreta Faber, who agreed to travel from Washington, D.C. for the occasion. Momentum was picking up. Next on the list was a call to the Anti-Defamation League in Boca Raton, to gauge their interest in supporting the Sarasota event. I wanted the ADL to present an honorary award to the ambassador as a thank you to the people of Albania for the country's role in saving Jews during World War II. ADL officials readily accepted my invitation and committed to attending and presenting the award to Ambassador Faber.

Fully nine months later, I finally completed my work spearheading the effort to hold the first International Holocaust Remembrance Day in Sarasota, Florida. Along the way, I eagerly agreed to continue volunteering with the Jewish Federation to organize and hold the event for years to come.

I spent my years with the Jewish Federation reaching out to and working with many fine nonprofit organizations that were in need of exposure and represented many worthy causes. In 2019, we at the Jewish Federation honored the Italian community, and in 2020, the Greek community, which had never been far from my heart. I decided to work with the Greeks to honor notable Greek leaders and their accomplishments. I quickly went into motion, doing what I do best, which is to organize and raise money. First, I recruited a special speaker, my cousin Dr. Mimis Cohen, who is a professor of plastic and reconstructive surgery at the University of Chicago. Next, I arranged for Greek dancers and some Greek food, especially the Greek pastry baklava, known everywhere for its delectable mix of honey, nuts, and cinnamon. Not surprisingly, that portion of my request was easy to fulfill. As another draw for the event, I looked up the Greek consul general in Tampa, Dimitrios Sparos, to arrange an appearance. Without much prodding, the veteran diplomat readily agreed to come, and he delivered a crowd-pleasing speech on Holocaust Remembrance Day.

Next, I arranged with Saint Barbara Church to show a 2013 documentary, *Song of Life,* directed by Irene Langemann, that detailed the history of the ancient island of Zakynthos in the Ionian Sea. The film takes place in 1943, during the Nazi occupation of Greece, when Mayor Loukas Karrer (along with the Greek Orthodox Bishop Chrysostomos) of Zakynthos refused Nazi orders to submit a list of the members of the town's Jewish community for deportation to the death camps. In all, the two men were instrumental in saving as many as 275 Jews who lived on the island, most of whom later moved safely to Israel or Athens. In fact, in 1978, Yad Vashem, the Holocaust Martyrs' and Heroes' Remembrance Authority in Israel, honored the bishop and the mayor with the title "Righteous Among the Nations," a specially minted medal reserved for non-Jews who, at great personal risk, saved Jews during the Holocaust. The men's names were also enshrined on the Wall of Honor in the Garden of the Righteous at Yad Vashem in Jerusalem.

A second documentary film, *Kisses to the Children,* directed by Vassilis Loules and released in 2011, was also shown. *Kisses* looks at the story of five Greek Jewish children – Rosina, Iossif, Eftyhia, Shelly, and Marios – who were saved by Christian families during the German occupation.

In all, the viewings were compelling, as were the baklava and other pastries, some of it sold by me personally at the Saint Barbara event. I love to volunteer during my spare time. It fulfills me. My life is happy because giving back is what I do. Helping others keeps me happy and young.

Even though some chapters in my life may have begun winding down, I have maintained my energetic volunteerism in support of women. In 2019, I organized combined celebrations for the Florida Chapter of International Women's Day and Albanian Teachers Day at the East Bay Country Club in Largo, Florida. Imelda Pojani was recognized with a Community Service Award in an event that drew 150 people and featured live music from Ermira Babaliu accompanied by Serafin Daka Organo. No single teacher was recognized that year, but instead I honored Albanian teachers who were no longer alive. I included my own teacher from elementary school in Vlora, Evrinomi Skufa, for special mention. Six-year-old Pandora Dervishi led the traditional mother's sing-along and more than $500 was collected via raffle to aid a needy Albanian American single mother living in Largo.

At one time I had the idea of naming my adopted hometown of Sarasota a sister city with my original hometown of Vlora. However, I found out that distinction had already gone to Hollywood, Florida. During my discussion with Dritan Leli, the mayor of Vlora, I discovered that along with the International Monetary Fund, work had begun on the reconstruction of the old city of Vlora with the idea of restoring it to its 1960s form. I immediately wrote to my relatives in Albania, Israel, and the US, and asked them to begin assembling items and documents for display in what would be Albania's first and only Jewish Museum. I contacted Mayor Leli, and was excited to find that the project, in a city that dates to the 15th century and the Spanish Inquisition, was already almost half completed in what has become the most Muslim and at the same time secular Islamic country in Europe. Vlora is also home to the only synagogue in Albania, although it is said that Jews no longer live there and perhaps only 100 Jews remain in the entire country of three million. Even at its peak, there were only a few hundred Jews in Albania.

I have never fully understood why others fail to step up with anything approaching my level of interest in Albania and in Albanian American affairs. It's strange how you always have some people who jump up and do things and then you have many others who go to sleep and do nothing. I have always felt ready to jump up, to participate, and to give whatever I could for the people and causes I believe in. I could write a whole book about my involvement with the AAWO over nearly 30 years – and maybe someday I will – such was my involvement and the many things that we managed to achieve.

24

2013, RETIREMENT

In December 2012, Markus and I decided it was time to sell my beloved practice to another dentist, along with my office, and put our apartment up for sale in preparation for retirement. I found a buyer for the practice I had built from scratch, coincidentally a Canadian of Greek origin, but just when he was to take over, he lost his mother and needed some time away. Our arrangement seemed otherwise ideal, and I understood his predicament. To smooth the transition, I agreed to work another month or two, to give him time to deal with his family affairs. When he returned, I was glad to see that he was able to pick up a significant number of my Greek American patients, and as per our agreement with the sale, I did not inform my patients that I was retiring. Rather, the new dentist was supposed to send a letter to my patient mailing list, explaining that the practice had been sold and introducing himself. Before long, however, I realized that he had not sent out the letter. Since I was still seeing patients just as I always had, albeit temporarily while he attended to the loss of his mother, it began to look as if nothing had changed. I felt uncomfortable as I treated my patients without telling them that I would soon be leaving.

I was so upset by this. I told him that I would only work for two more weeks, and at the end of January I would be finished. I really did not want to keep my extending my stay as if I were still the owner. He told me he had been busy with my office and another one he owned, but I felt like I was not being truthful to my beloved patients. We had an honest family practice, and our entire staff was so close with everyone who came to us, many patients had been with us for decades. I had always discussed many personal things with my patients, and they had trusted me with their confidences and secrets.

But finally, the deal closed, and the new dentist took over. I left my patients and my old practice behind. At last, it was time for what many New Yorkers know as the "inevitable move to Florida," the classic retirement destination. Markus and I first tried Florida's east coast where some friends had preceded us in retirement. We looked for a place in South Beach, the sometimes-riotous part of Miami Beach, but felt that the younger lifestyle there didn't suit us (even though Markus loved to take after-dinner walks in that area). But that wasn't enough to lure us. *Better to visit than live there,* we thought. The somewhat more sedate North Beach area failed to yield a suitable home either. It was time to recalibrate our search.

We flew back to New York and prepared to sell our co-op apartment on the Upper East Side. In June 2013, we listed the apartment and headed off to Israel to visit relatives, particularly Markus' son Alan and his family with whom we were very close. It was wonderful to spend time with Alan's three children: Yasmin, Gidon, and Yiar. We did not see Markus' daughter, Deenah, who also lives in Israel, because unfortunately, they are not close.

Over the years, we spent weekends at our summerhouse in Woodstock in upstate New York. Markus' children would often visit from Israel and New York, along with their families, and the time away from the city allowed the entire family to make many wonderful memories. Everyone loved hiking in the Catskills, and we did it often. We would leave the house early in the morning and not come back until night! These were such wonderful, happy times. We used to travel to Israel a lot around that time, too.

But after working for nearly half a century, I longed for the vacation I'd never really had and now it was our time to go to Israel and relax. So, we flew to Tel Aviv and stayed with Alan, his wife Dr.

Yael Arbel-De Rowe (a gynecologist in Netanya and daughter of a war hero), and their children for six weeks in Moshav Sal'it in the West Bank not far from Tel Aviv.

Alan's family continued their normal activities during our visit, so Markus and I created a schedule. Early each morning, he set out to walk the family dog and I did the laundry. At 10 a.m., we drove to the beach an hour away to swim and have lunch. When we returned around 3 p.m., I folded the clean clothes from the clothesline and put everything away. This was followed by a short break and perhaps a quick nap before Alan and Yael returned from work. Yael is a wonderful cook so she would make dinner, and I would do the dishes. I organized everything and gave everyone a little job to do. We had such a great time together. On the weekends when Alan and Yael were free, we would go for short trips with them and their children. This was unquestionably a vacation designed for relaxation.

Finally, the time came for Markus and I to return to the US. After all, we had a house to sell, and I was now ready to resume fundraising efforts to mark the 20th anniversary of the AAWO. The six weeks in Sal'it, as pleasurable and peaceful as they were, eventually gave way to stateside commitments. It was time to say our goodbyes. The day we were leaving, Yael gave us each a big hug and a kiss. Then she said to me, from a daughter-in-law to a mother-in-law, "Please don't go. Just stay here with us six months and then go back and sell your house. Don't go anywhere else. Just always stay with us." And with that, she turned and ran back into the house! She couldn't bear to say goodbye. She came back three times to attempt a proper goodbye, but each time she became so overcome that she had to turn and run into the house again. Her display of her true emotions was so touching, and far more meaningful than any words of goodbye could ever be. She showed her father and me so much love in those moments, love we are so grateful for and cherish deeply. But it was time for us to go, and with full hearts from our wonderful visit, we made our way to the airport.

Back in New York, we began to pack our belongings in anticipation of the sale. There was so much to do. In May 2014, almost a year after it was listed, our apartment in Manhattan was sold. There was no turning back now! The next chapter of our lives was ahead of us, and the road looked smooth. By this point, we had given up on south Florida and decided upon Sarasota, about an hour south of Tampa on the state's more placid West coast. There was, however, one minor snag: I did not want to leave New York. I was hysterical about it. I didn't want to go to Sarasota. I wanted to buy a studio apartment in New York. In that way we could keep our place in Woodstock along with the studio in New York and we could travel back and forth between the two and see our kids and our friends.

But Markus persisted and eventually he persuaded me to visit Sarasota for a week to see for myself and give the city a reasonable try. I had been there once before, briefly, and spent a little time on Siesta Key Beach, which had appealed to me. After all, Vlora, where I grew up, also had a gorgeous beach. The weeklong tryout worked. We enjoyed the visit, and I was now convinced that I was ready to move to Sarasota. We moved quickly and with the help of a local realtor and our son, Olek, we found a spacious condominium apartment not on the beach, but downtown with a spectacular view of Sarasota Bay. Within the space of that week, we arranged to buy the condo and move from New York.

The wheels were most definitely in motion for our move to Florida. But there was the lingering matter of the Woodstock home, technically in nearby Saugerties, New York, which we had owned for 32 years. During that time, we had enjoyed and shared numerous Thanksgiving holidays with multitudes of friends and relatives. We had made some great memories in that house. Now, in 2014, we would celebrate our last Thanksgiving there, because we had finally decided to sell it. We just weren't using it any longer. The kids' lives were not conducive to using it either, so we felt it was time to give it up.

In December, our daughter Felicia, who still lived in New York, was due to give birth and I grew concerned that she might have trouble concentrating, what with her having to stop her work at the fashion company, Guess, and not having Markus and I available as her support system. I floated the idea of having Felicia join us in Sarasota, where we could help her with the baby, who we wanted to have near us, of course. She agreed and in May 2015, she moved to Sarasota with our granddaughter, Alana. Felicia was a single mother now and the two of them stayed with us for a short time, until she rented an apartment for herself and the baby nearby.

There were still a few more pieces of my retirement puzzle to work out. On Valentine's Day 2015, at the Sarasota Yacht Club, Olek married his girlfriend, Caitlin, who is actually a native of Sarasota who migrated north to New York. They made their home in Pelham, New York, just north of the city, and soon welcomed their first child, a son named Alex. A second son, Dylan, was born in May of 2019. With close ties to Sarasota because we live here and Caitlin is from here, we have enjoyed annual visits from Olek and his beautiful family over the years.

The way in which Olek and Caitlin met was itself a series of coincidences that started in 2012, when I put my dental office up for sale. A couple were very interested and were about to buy the office, but the sale fell through because they refused to pay a down payment before the closing. I had high hopes for the sale, but once the deal collapsed, I grew depressed. The entire sale process would have to be restarted. That week I was called for jury duty and soon walked into a crowded Manhattan courthouse and noticed a pretty blonde woman sitting alone on one of the benches that are reserved for potential jurors. I sat down next to her, exchanged polite hellos, and began to fill out juror forms. Then I noticed her name was Caitlin Weiner. I thought, *Oh my God, she's Jewish and beautiful.* Eager to pass the time, we began to chat, and when I asked where she was from, she replied, "Sarasota, Florida." I told her that my husband loved Sarasota and wanted us to move there. During the course of our conversation, I mentioned that I was from Albania and that my parents were from Greece. Caitlin told me that she had been living in New York for less than three years and that she had recently dated a Greek man, but they had just broken up.

Her response instantly caused me, forever the Jewish mother, to probe my new friend a bit further, "Oh?" I asked. "Do you have a new boyfriend?" Caitlin said no. I then asked where she lived, and it turned out that Caitlin lived just about ten blocks from Markus and me. We were both surprised. "Well then," Caitlin said. "Maybe once we're finished with jury duty, we can take the subway together back to the Upper East Side."

At that point I had a confession to make. I told her a bit sheepishly that I was a Jewish princess and didn't take the subway, and that my husband usually picked me up and dropped me off wherever I went. Anyway, Markus had dropped me off in our car at the courthouse in lower Manhattan that morning and would be waiting to pick me up. I suggested the three of us go out for lunch in nearby Chinatown. Caitlin agreed.

Perhaps there was something extra in the dim sum that day, but the lunch could not have gone better. The three of us talked and laughed and enjoyed each other's company immensely. She was so beautiful, sweet, and nice. She hugged Markus warmly and thanked us for lunch. We all had an incredible time. Markus was struck with her kindness and genuine feelings. We were both blown away.

Lunch ended and it was time to return to the courthouse since neither of us had yet been released from jury obligation. On the way back I overheard Caitlin talking on the phone with a coworker, raving about the wonderful time she was having and how she had befriended a woman who was a dentist. "Maybe she'll be my dentist," she told her friend.

A phone call to Caitlin the next day was my chance to step up my game and move to Phase Two. I said to her that I had a son who was close to her age and maybe she could meet up with him and his friends sometime, through them maybe she would meet someone. I was not trying to set them up. I just left it to open. I did, however, offer to throw in Olek's email address and suggested that perhaps they could meet on Facebook, even though I admitted to Caitlin that I didn't know how Facebook worked. It just sounded like a good idea.

For his part, Olek (who was single, handsome, smart, and a top executive in the commercial real estate section of The Bancorp in Manhattan), was having little trouble meeting people, especially women. This came as no surprise to us. Even New York Mayor Michael Bloomberg's sister had a daughter she thought might be right for Olek. It wasn't to be, however. But when Markus and I talked up Caitlin to our son, he at least listened, although as far as I knew that was where it ended. Just talk.

Time passed and about three months later when it came time for a family dinner, which I prepared every two weeks or so to at least see our kids and catch up with their lives, Olek said that someone would be joining him. I asked who and he said, "Caitlin." He told me that they had been going out and that it was going very well. I was pleased, if not ecstatic, and I had a hard time concealing my feelings about this development. The dinner went very well, mainly because Markus and I already knew and liked Olek's guest! We reminisced about our delightful lunch in Chinatown, and how our meeting that day made even jury duty fun.

Olek and Caitlin kept dating, then moved in together in his New York apartment, and later married in a big ceremony in Sarasota. What a coincidence, the strange way things happen. We thought our family connections would always center around New York, even after retirement, but instead we gained a daughter-in-law with ties to Sarasota. It was all so wonderful. They're very happy and we're very happy for them. They still live in New York, but we see them a few times a year, which is wonderful. In fact, it's great. It's life!

The pieces of the puzzle didn't come together quite as smoothly for Felicia. In December 2014, she gave birth to her daughter, Alana. But Felicia and her boyfriend never married and unfortunately her boyfriend became an ex-boyfriend. Markus and I were very worried about the situation but were very grateful and relieved once our daughter and granddaughter relocated to Sarasota.

Felicia and Alana still live close by, which is a boon to us proud and happy grandparents, of course. Alana is growing up to be a beautiful little girl with an old, wise soul and the thoughtfulness of someone many years her senior. On top of this, she cracks us up with her quick wit and unique sense of humor. She has her good moments and her bad moments, but the good moments are so beautiful. Alana goes to a Hebrew school and most of all she loves going to the synagogue with her grandpa. That's her favorite thing. By age four she was attending school five days a week at Temple Emanuel in Sarasota, where Felicia teaches Hebrew in Sunday school. Alana also spends three or four nights each week with us, Nona and Papu. But what makes me even more excited for her is the fact that Alana is learning Hebrew and from age four has been able to count and even recite the Shabbat prayers in Hebrew.

During Passover 2018, when Markus went to temple wearing his tallit, he stood up and prayed. Alana followed his lead and stood up, too. Whatever her Papu did, she did. At one point she got under his tallit and Markus was so proud and happy to be with her. She reminded him that as a child in Poland, he went under the tallit of his father. Markus feels so blessed by having Alana in his life. He often tells me, "I'm living for her."

Two years after moving to Florida, in January 2015, Markus began experiencing problems with his kidneys, and it soon became apparent that he would need dialysis. It was the beginning of a difficult physical struggle for him, and it also took a psychological toll on me. Reading about his health issues and thinking about what it all meant was very painful for me. I'm the type of person who takes everyone's struggles upon myself. I have always had strong feelings about needing to help others and with that comes a lot of worry. I care more for others than I do about myself – it has just always been my way to put myself last. So, when the doctor said Markus had to start dialysis treatments, we were devastated. I especially worried that my husband and I would no longer be able to travel as we had long planned. It was at that point that we made the decision to sell our home in Saugerties, near Woodstock.

Then something of a miracle took place. Two years into his three-days-per-week dialysis regimen, Markus began to regain strength. Soon after that, however, he was diagnosed with prostate cancer. Despite the new cancer diagnosis, his checkups were positive, his attitude and prognosis were excellent, and his health was decidedly improving. After a trying period, things were looking up and my worries abated.

Markus has his own story to tell, a personal story from when he was a child. He is from Dembica, a Jewish shtetl in southeastern Poland, about 100 km (62 m) east of Krakow. He was born in 1934, the first of two sons of the Orthodox, Yiddish-speaking Solomon Derszowicz and Fela Schus. His younger brother Asher – who everyone called Olek – was two years younger than him. His parents owned a fabrics business in the center of Dembica, lived in the apartments above the store, and the town was full of Fela's family, who were merchants. Solomon and Fela were upper middle class, had two Polish servants, and as Markus likes to say, "It was just like *Fiddler on the Roof.*"

It is best to record here in his own words what happened to him, his brother, and the Jews of Dembica:

"I was six years old when the Nazis invaded. My curse is to remember everything perfectly. A plane dropped a bomb on the local brickworks, and we kids ran to take a look. Then people said to go and see the Polish Army garrison. When we got there none of the planes had their propellers. They had been sabotaged. It was September 1939, and the Nazi blitzkrieg was on. By January 1940, all the Jews had to go into the Dembica ghetto. My father's parents were brought from where they lived in Przecław on a cattle car and spent one night with us before being sent to Auschwitz. The Nazis were bringing Jews from all the surrounding villages to Dembica and then sending them to Auschwitz. Of course we did not know it was a death camp. Everybody said they were being sent to work camps.

"My mother's younger sister got married just before the war, her husband was an engineer, and they were brought to our ghetto. My uncle managed to escape a transport. He came back to the ghetto and started screaming, 'These are not work camps, they are gassing you, they are killing you!' Everybody thought he had lost his mind, and nobody believed him. They treated him like he was an idiot. He ended up killing himself.

"When the Nazis liquidated the Dembica ghetto in July 1943, we were on the last train: my father, mother, brother and hundreds of other people. It was a cattle car, they just pushed us in. They took us on more than a 100-km journey. When we stopped, we were at Auschwitz. There were a lot of sidings – eight sidings – and wagons from all over the country being unloaded. We stayed in the car that night, and the whole next day. The second night, my father said, 'This is not a work camp.' You could smell the burning flesh. My father pried up the boards on the floor and pushed my brother and my mother and me through the hole, and then squeezed through it himself. No one else wanted to escape with us. They said, 'They'll kill you if you run away.' But my father knew they would kill us anyway.

"My father knew where Jewish partisans were in the nearby Beskid Mountains, maybe 70–80 km (40–50 m) away. It took us three days and we walked only at night. We finally got to where the partisans were, but they would not take children because kids couldn't be trusted to not make noise. They were in lean-tos in the forest, some of them had guns—but not all—and they were surviving by stealing or buying food from the local farmers. They allowed us to stay there for two days. My father left my mother with the partisans, and he walked my brother and me down to a small village named Brzeziny. There was no electricity, no nothing. He knew someone there, I don't know the connection, and he gave that man some diamonds or something valuable. That family would not keep two kids, but they would keep one. Since I was the same age as one of the daughters, they took me and decided that my brother would go to the wife's parents, who had the farm up the road. The homes in that region – the Galicia region – were spread far apart. Each farmhouse was far from any other. The Polish farmer's house had three rooms, one room for the cows and pigs, a second room for the kitchen and dining and living room, and the third room where the family slept. My father left me with that family – I do not recall their names – and then he left with the farmer's wife and my brother to take him to her parents. Those farmers were taking a very big risk, but they were paid for it.

"That family had two daughters, one was exactly my age, almost the same birthday, and the other was a little younger. I had blue eyes and looked just like them. I liked them. They called me my Polish name, Mietek, a very common name. I slept in the hay in the loft in the animals' room. I would hide there when any neighbors would come by. I was not to be seen at all by anyone. I never went more than ten feet away from the house and I was there seven or eight months. I just felt numb because of everything that had happened. The farmer put me to work cleaning after the animals. Very rarely did I ever sit with them for a meal. I used to steal the eggs from the chickens and eat them raw.

"The wife's parents had two buildings, a house and a separate barn, so they must have been wealthy for that area. They were probably in their late 50s, early 60s, too old to have a young child like my brother. Somebody must have told the Nazis that there were Jews hiding there. One night the farmer came running, grabbed me, took me into their bedroom, and threw me into their bed. A half-track was coming. It was so quiet there, you could hear the half-tracks even when they were many miles away. Six Nazis came with flashlights. I saw them, I counted them. I was scared. They were screaming in German. After screaming, screaming, screaming, they left. As soon as they left, the farmer threw me out the window. Not pushed me. He threw me out. He was screaming, 'Just go!' I was eight years old.

"I started walking to where my brother was. It was about a half mile. By the time I got there, I saw that the Germans had him up against the barn wall, they had the headlights of the half-track on him, and then they machine-gunned him right in front of me. I got so pissed, I started throwing rocks at them. I was hiding in a cornfield, and they couldn't see me, but they started shooting at me anyway. I will never forget the sound of the bullets going by. It was like a game to me. I threw the rocks, they shot bullets. They tried to turn the headlights of the half-track on me, but even with the headlights, they could not see me. They searched for me for a long time and then finally gave up. I started walking to where my parents were.

"I walked for four days and four nights, and I found them. I told them I saw my brother shot and that he was dead. That's when my father decided we could not stay with the partisans. We walked back to Dembica. My father knew a Polish family on the outskirts of town whose daughter married a Jewish lawyer who had converted to Catholicism but ended up at Auschwitz anyway. My father made a deal with that family that if we survived the war, he would give them our house. He signed over the papers then and there. We knew the

Germans were not doing so well, that the Russians were coming, and that maybe the war would not last much longer.

"The Polish family had dug a hole under their pantry and the three of us hid there. I could sit up in it, but my parents could not. When we slept, if one of us turned, all of us had to turn. We had a bucket for our toilet. They let us out every two days just so we could straighten out our bodies a little bit. We did that for six months.

"After the Russians came in November 1944, the war was over for us. Dembica became the winter headquarters of the First Belorussian Army. We went into the town and stayed at our house. The Germans had occupied it, used our home as their living quarters and the store below as their offices. After the war ended, my mother went to that farmhouse where my brother was murdered. She dug up my brother's body, brought it home and buried it in the cemetery in Dembica.

"I remember so many vivid images. I remember throwing rocks over the high wall of the ghetto and the Polish kids throwing rocks back. I remember Germans beating people, being very sick when I was hiding in that hole and having such a high fever that I felt like I was falling. I have a heart murmur to this day because of that. After the war, I was malnourished, and I would fall and skin my knees and the wounds would not heal. My father found a female Russian doctor, an army colonel who spoke Polish, and she treated me with two different ointments, one yellow and one black. I fell in love with her.

"We had to leave Dembica because the family that hid us in the pantry owned our house now. My father decided that we were going to America. He had an uncle there, my grandfather's brother, Irving Dersh. He'd left in 1922 and changed his name. He owned a blouse factory on Lower Broadway. My mother also had some cousins in America who were quite wealthy. We left Dembica, were smuggled to Vienna and went to the Rothschild Hospital, which was a refugee center. They sprayed me with DDT to delouse me. HIAS took care of us after that. They put us in a Displaced Persons camp where we stayed awhile, and then my father wanted to go to the American Zone in Germany, and we ended up in a DP camp in Bad Reichenhall, where there were former army barracks. We were there for four years and my sister Helen was born there in 1949. My parents had been able to connect with our family in the United States through HIAS, and we got a lot of things from my father's uncle that we could sell for money.

"My father hired two professors from the local high school to teach me, one for science and one for language and social studies. After one year of studying with them, they felt I was ready to go to the high school. I was the only refugee, the only Polack, the only Jew, going to the high school in Bad Reichenhall. After that year, my father hired the professors again. I took a year off school and studied with them, and I passed the exams and was admitted to the final year of high school.

"Going to school with Germans was awful. The other students used to call me names, beat me up. They were big, and some of them had been in the war. They would gang up on me and I would go into a kind of hibernation to get through it. I would clean myself up before going home because I was afraid that my parents would stop sending me to the school if they knew. But in the evenings, if I would catch one of them alone in the town, I would beat the hell out of him. I learned how to fight.

"We arrived in the United States on July 26, 1950, on the USS General Hahn, an army transport. We anchored right off Coney Island, and I was up all night looking at the lights. We went to HIAS on Lafayette Street and were there for two weeks. My uncle and father found an apartment in Brooklyn for us, and in the beginning of August, I went to Lincoln High School with my German papers, but they decided I didn't speak English well enough to be admitted. The assistant principal knew German, she told me as they were walking me out, 'You may not be able to go to high school, but you can go to college. My friend is the Dean of Admissions at Brooklyn College.' I went there the next day, got admitted. Dean Adele Bildersee. I'll never forget her name. I was 15 and a half. I laughed at how ridiculous it was that I could go to college but not high school. I thought, *What kind of country is this?* I finished college in two and a half years.

"I never philosophized about my experiences. I knew it made me different than other people. All through high school and college, I lived with a fantasy. I remember in 1945 when the Americans dropped the atom bomb on Japan, I decided I was going to build an atom bomb and drop it on Germany to get even for my brother. I got up in the morning with that fantasy, I went to bed with that fantasy. When I finished college, I went to Columbia University because I'd read that the Manhattan Project had been there. And one of the main people involved in the project was Dr. Isidor Isaac Rabi, who was originally from Romanov on the Polish-Hungarian border. I found his office. It was lunchtime and the secretary was out. I heard him talking on his phone in Yiddish. When he finished his call, we started talking in Yiddish. Before you knew it, I was enrolled and had an assistantship. I told him I wanted to build an atom bomb and he said, 'Ok, you want to build an atom bomb.' I worked in the laboratories downstairs, and on Fridays I would have dinner at his house and his wife loved me. Oppenheimer came occasionally; he talked me out of it. He told me, 'If you really want to do that, the only people you can work for is the government.' He wasn't allowed to read his own work at that time because he had been accused of being a communist and had lost his security clearance.

"It's human nature to think of revenge. It's one of the basic human instincts. When I saw my brother get killed with the machine guns, with the headlights of the half-track shining on him, this desire for revenge lived with me until 1955. It was my mission in life to get even. I suffered the German high school just to build an atom bomb. I never even thought about how I would steal an airplane, let alone fly it, to drop a bomb on Germany. It was irrational and peculiar.

"I became a US citizen in 1955, and right after I got my citizenship papers, I changed my last name to De Rowe. In college, no one could spell Derszowicz or pronounce it. My cousin in France changed our name to Dersot, my uncle had changed it to Dersh, a cousin in Chicago had changed it to Dero. I wrote down De Rowe and decided that was how I was going to change it. My father never changed his name. As for my mother, the trauma eventually caused her to lose her mind."

Markus used to get physically ill when he would try to watch Holocaust films like *Schindler's List* and *The Pianist*, and he would become unable to breathe. He has only been able to talk about his experiences in recent years, which he has done at a number of celebrations and events. On one such occasion, a representative of the Florida Holocaust Museum in St. Petersburg invited him to be formally interviewed. The resulting interview was video recorded and, along with a personal collection of photographs, has become part of the permanent collection at the museum.

25

BESA, THE MORAL CODE, AS A LESSON FOR HUMANITY

I have received many awards over the years – many coming from Albanian organizations – and I am so extremely grateful and appreciative of the accolades and recognition. In January 2004, I received the Special Merit award from the president of Albania for helping the Albanian people during the humanitarian crisis in Kosovo and for aiding new immigrants who emigrated to the US. In 2006, I renamed the Albanian street where most Jews lived – the street everyone used to call *Rruga e Çifutëve* (The Street of the Jews), which was very derogatory – with a new moniker that honors and respects the Jewish culture and the families who lived there, *Rruga e Ebrenjëve* (The Jewish Street). That same year, I was given the title of Honored Citizen of Vlora. In 2016, I received the Gold Eagle Diaspora Award on behalf of the AAWO.

In November of 2019, The Jewish Federation of Sarasota/Manatee honored me with a special plaque and a tree planted in Israel in my honor, for my volunteer work and annual organizing of the International Holocaust Remembrance Day events. I continue to work on Holocaust Remembrance Day activities with this wonderful organization, which are particularly meaningful since my husband, Markus, is a child Holocaust survivor.

Around that same time in 2019, along with wonderful people like

Gail Shirazi, Evie Stroller, and the Kosovar-Jewish diplomat, Ines Demiri, we organized a very special event in Potomac, Maryland. The event, which took place Sunday, November 17, was held in a packed conference hall in Congregation B'nai Tzedek, where literally hundreds of people took part, including congregants, scholars, journalists, historians, politicians, businesspeople, and many Albanian Americans. The evening was sponsored by the Friends of the Jewish Museum of Kosovo, the American Sephardi Federation, the Embassy of Kosovo, and the B'nai Tzedek Congregation. Pianist Merzana Kostreci played *Lule Bore* among other wonderful pieces, and introductory remarks were delivered by Frymëzim Isufaj, Charge D'Affairs of the Embassy of Republic of Kosovo in Washington, D.C. The Albanian Ambassador to the US, Floreta Faber, also spoke beautifully.

Following the speeches, the documentary film *The Righteous Gypsy* was shown. The film highlighted the heroic, lifesaving work of Hajrija Imeri-Mihaljić, a Roma woman from the village of Ade, who rescued from the Nazis and raised as her own a young girl named Esther Levy. The event also included a presentation to George Preng Uli in honor of his father's heroism rescuing Jews during World War II. This award was designed by Masha Roth of Sarasota.

After those important events, I flew to New York where the city's first ever celebration of Albanian independence was held. That event took place November 21, 2019, at City Hall in Manhattan, and was organized by Mark Gjonaj, the Albanian American councilman from the Bronx. It honored people from Macedonia, Kosovo, and Chameria – a region in southern Albania – as well as people of Greek Muslim origin who moved to Albania and assimilated there. And Albania itself was celebrated. It was with great pride that I represented Albania that day. I was thrilled to be involved with this event for many reasons. Independence for Albania began in my hometown of Vlora. In my short speech that day, I pointed out that I felt very honored, particularly since I was born in Vlora. The Albanian flag was first raised there. I'm an honored citizen of Vlora, and the Jews of Vlora took part in the independence of Albania.

Here is the text of the speech I gave that day:

Speaker Corey Johnson, City Council members, Councilman Mark Gjonaj, members of the Albanian and Jewish communities, honorees Motra e Vllezër (Sisters and Brothers),

I am so humbled and honored to be here today, celebrating with all of you the 106th year of Albanian independence from the Ottoman Empire. The flag of the Declaration of Independence was raised by Albanian diplomat Ismail Qemali on November 28, 1912, in the city of Vlora, the same city where I was lucky to have been born from Greek Jewish parents. I hold with pride the honored citizens of Vlora.

Besides Albanians, many local Jews also participated in the struggle for the independence of Albania. After the declaration of independence, leader Ismail Qemali and friends went to the Kantozi Jewish family to celebrate.

We are so lucky to have one of our own on the city council here in New York. Therefore, we recognize council Mark Gjonaj, who made this event possible. Now, we celebrate Albanian independence in our historic New York City Hall. A special thank you, Mr. Gjonaj, for what you do for all the communities that you represent in your district.

Last but not least, I would like to congratulate all of tonight's honorees. Happy independence, Albania. I am honored to represent you.

Gezuar festen e flamurit! Thank you!

And earlier that year, on January 31, 2019, I was invited to give the most important speech of my life, a very powerful speech to the General Assembly of the United Nations, the text of which I have provided here:

Good afternoon, ladies and gentlemen,
   Motra e Vllezër (Sisters and Brothers)

I am very humbled to be here today to speak about the generosity and humanity to the Jewish people by the Albanians during World War II.

In remembering the Holocaust, we look back on these dark times of civilization with tearful eyes and broken hearts, trying to find lighter moments to ease the pain.

Every tragedy has its own good side. It brings people together, regardless of race or religion. It tries to restore hope in the victims' soul and attempts to heal the wounds inflicted upon them by their fellow human beings.

The Holocaust is not only going to be remembered for the millions of lives that perished into the flames of hatred, but it will also be remembered for the humanity of others helping the Jewish people.

There is a small country in Europe called Albania, where I was fortunately born, where hospitality to foreigners is part of their tradition.

During the war, not only did Albanians save the Jews, but they shared their home, souls, food, and lives with them.

My family was one of many saved.

I am not a survivor, but a child of survivors; born in the ancient city of Vlora.

In 1492, during the Spanish Inquisition, many Sephardic Jews settled in this city, and the total number of Jewish families was 528 out of 945.

In 1938 there were only 15 Jewish families.

In 1991, most of the Jews of Albania went to Israel and 37 people came to the US with my help.

These are my relatives.

My parents, Nina and David Kohen and my grandparents Elia and Anetta Kohen came from Ioannina, Greece. They lived in the city of Vlora, and when the Nazis invaded Albania, they fled to the mountains and hid in a small Muslim village called Trevllazër. They changed their names to Muslim names.

My grandmother Anetta became Fatima, and my grandfather Elia became Ali. My father's name of David became Daut, and my mother's name of Nina became Bule.

Everyone in the village knew they were Jews, but no one betrayed them.

I have a very interesting personal experience to share with you. When I was about 5 or 6 years old, I was walking down our street with my mother, and I heard someone shouting "Bule! Bule!" I turned my head to see what was going on and a woman was running toward us. She ran to my mother and started to kiss and hug her, with tears streaming down her face. I was stunned. I did not know who this woman was and why they were hugging each other. Later on, my mother told me that she was one of the women from the Muslim village that had saved their lives.

In 2005 I was instrumental in renaming the street that all Jewish families resided on in Vlora to "The Jewish Street," and installed a plaque with all the names of the Jews that lived on that street, including me and my family. Today it is a tourist attraction.

As you can see, the Albanian people risked their own lives for the Jewish people.

I would not be here today, delivering this speech, if not for the courage and generosity of the people of Albania, who took us among themselves and made us feel at home, not like hunted animals.

All Jews, most of them not Albanian citizens, were saved within Albanian borders. Albania was the only country in Europe where the Jewish population was much larger at the end of the war than before.

Jews did not suffer, because Albanians everywhere in Southeast Europe concealed and took care of them at great personal risk. The salvation in Albania was TOTAL, and without interruption.

It was an entire culture that resisted the Holocaust and saved all Jews within its reach, a combined result of the deeds of the Kingdom of Albania and a population with deep roots in the tradition of harmony, tolerance, and Besa.

What is Besa? Besa is a moral code, a norm of social behavior, a promise. Besa is an ancient protocol of the Albanian society, in which only the concept of a guest exists, and not that of the foreigner.

The Albanians were not silent, they did not look away, they were not indifferent.

May this day be not only an act of remembrance, but a remembrance to ACT.

To act on behalf of any individual, or political, religious, or ethnic group that is being attacked and dehumanized.

As Elie Wiesel said, "Not all victims were Jews, but all Jews were victims."

I ask you today, never to condemn an entire people, culture, or religion, but to see each person individually, and to treat them all with the tolerance and respect they deserve.

Each person has a name and an identity. Each person is a Universe. As we say in the Talmud: "He who saved a life has saved the world entire."

Though there is evil, see the goodness in others who wish to live among us in peace and harmony.

Let me share with you an act of humanity between an Arab and a Jew: Mohammed and Myself. Mohammed had a coffee cart right across from my office on 63rd street and Lexington in Manhattan. Every morning, I bought coffee and we exchanged conversation, shared family events, a newborn baby, a happy, hard-working family.

The day after 9/11, a lot of vendors like Muhammed were vandalized, their carts destroyed.

I immediately took action, as I feared for Mohammed. I did not want him to get hurt, so I put a large American flag on his cart, without his knowing, and taped it down. When he turned and saw me, we both had tears in our eyes. He came out of his cart and hugged me and thanked me.

We had a connection – a wish for harmony, humanity, and peace among peoples.

We the people have a commitment ... to remember the victims who perished, respect the survivors still with us, and reaffirm humanity's common aspiration for mutual understanding and justice. We should Never Forget.

Helen Borstein, a 92-year-old Holocaust survivor from Poland, shared her story at an event that I recently attended. She mentioned that she had seen her doctor a day before this event, and he had no knowledge about the number that was tattooed on her arm.

It is appalling that many people all over the world, including in America, in this day and age, have absolutely no knowledge or understanding of the Holocaust.

On behalf of the Albanian Jews living in Albania, Israel, and America, and elsewhere, I would like to give a message to the Albanian people and the Righteous Gentiles:

Thank you for saving us. We will never forget you.

And as a testament to honoring your compassion and courage, we have just learned that the International Raoul Wallenberg Foundation has proclaimed the Republic of Albania as a House of Life, to commemorate the brave spirit and hospitality of the Albanian Rescuers under the tradition of Besa and has erected a plaque on the main garden across from the President's Building.

Such a beautiful and well-deserved tribute!

Thank you.

26

A RETROSPECTIVE LOOK AT LIFE

As a lifelong planner, I have never left a decision to chance, no matter how large or small. I have planned my life out from a young age. I'm a born planner. I planned to have a girl and a boy, and I did (I know you will think that was by chance, but I believe it was my planning). I planned to open my own dental office and I made it happen, right in the heart of New York City. I planned for each of the homes that have been my own since I could afford them, and Markus and I have enjoyed Manhattan, and the Bronx, and Woodstock through our years together.

The home we now share was another longstanding dream of mine, which was to own a house on the water. I put that dream off for decades, and sometimes it felt too out of reach, but eventually it came true. I was born in the city of Vlora – located on a beautiful bay – and now halfway around the world, in the city of Sarasota, I feel like I'm back there. We live on a gorgeous bay with a picturesque view of sailboats gliding by. It was my final dream that I desperately wanted to come true.

People ask me if I have any regrets. I do not have many. But there is one important one I do have. I wanted to complete one more year of medical school to become a physician, but never went back to Greece to finish my degree. I regret not doing that because I would have been able to help even more people, by treating and guiding my patients with their medical problems, in addition to their dental problems. I would have been an internist, not a specialist, for the same reasons I became a general dentist. I wanted to treat every aspect of my patients' issues, every tooth problem, not just some of them, or only one part of the mouth. In terms of my career, I especially loved the cosmetic aspect of dentistry. I was never happier than when I could end a patient's pain and give them the confidence of a beautiful smile.

Essentially, I became one of the fortunate few, able to live the life I aspired to. I reached my goals through hard work and perseverance, and never stopped caring about others. If I had 50 more years to live, I would still do what I have been doing all along: helping people, especially women and children. I would also keep organizing special events and helping fundraise for different nonprofits, which is doing what I love to do best.

If given more time, I also would travel. Markus' dialysis regimen made that nearly impossible, but that aside, I would like to take a cruise, something I have never experienced, in part because of my anxiety over becoming seasick.

When I think of some of the extraordinary times in my life, many of my valuable experiences and life lessons came from my father. Working with my father in Albania to convince the dictator, Enver Hoxha, to let our family leave meant so much to me. I was my father's secretary. We did the paperwork together, and our hard work paid off. We did get out of Albania, but we never forgot that beautiful country. And I am so grateful to have met the children of the Muslim Albanians in the mountains who saved my parent's and grandparent's lives.

I may have been the number two child, and female, but I was first to help my father when he needed me. I was a good listener. There were times my father would say something in his poor Albanian and I would correct it in the official letter writing. Then he would say, "Okay, now read it back to me," and I would. He would listen and ask me to add this or that. It took us hours and hours to write those letters, but we did it. Today, I'm the same person my father was. If I want to write a speech, it is easier for me to write it and then hear someone read it back to me rather than for me to read it back to myself. The letter to Hoxha worked not just because my father and I wrote it together, but because we worked very hard to write it perfectly. To leave Albania, we made many sacrifices as a family, and were lucky at the time to do so.

I also fondly recall a prediction I made when I was a young girl, one that shows how life can come full circle and that dreams really can come true. When I was young, I used to love to draw the bay of Vlora with the sun setting between the mountains on either side, framing that sparkling water. It was such a spectacular setting, and I always added a sailboat in the middle of the scene. The sailboat would have a Star of David on it, but the boat was always empty. I was hoping that one day this boat would be filled with Jewish tourists who had come to visit Albania and see my ancient city. Sure enough, today many Israelis do just that and make great holiday memories on the beautiful bay of Vlora.

27

IN CLOSING, SOME ADVICE

Now in my mid seventies, I feel content and satisfied with the way my life has turned out. I have accomplished almost everything I set out to do. I've done enough that I feel that I have used my ability to contribute to society in general and done good things for the Albanian and Jewish communities, and the communities I have lived in throughout my life. But due to my circumstances today, with Markus' need for dialysis, travel is altogether unfeasible. We can only dream and fantasize about the traveling we had hoped to do. But I am very pleased that I have been able to help those in need as well as those who are dearest and closest to me. And they know I am always there for them. I love to be a good friend to everyone. I love to help anyone I can and giving back makes me feel wonderful.

My life story and the stories of my parents and grandparents speak for themselves. But I want to leave these words for my grandchildren. First, if something doesn't happen just the way you want it to, say this, "There is a reason for everything. Everything happens for a reason." I want to tell my grandchildren to respect their parents and to respect themselves. I want them to choose professions they truly love because if they find themselves in professions that only chose for money, that cannot lead to lasting happiness. To be happy, you must do something that you love. That's why I chose the profession I did. I love to help people and I truly loved practicing dentistry. I don't think I could have helped as many people as I did in any other way.

I am also eager to tell my grandchildren that honesty is not just a virtue, it is a way of life. Don't be afraid to tell the truth. Sometimes it's not easy telling the truth and being honest may actually hurt you in the short term. But in the long run, you must tell the truth because the moment you begin to lie, you must continue with that same lie and that will make everyone and especially you miserable. Lying is never a choice we should make.

Parallel to the subject of honesty runs the question of human flaws and frailties. To be totally honest, people should be honest about themselves and concede their imperfections. A couple living together, married or not, should always share duties and neither one should try to do everything alone. I am the type who likes to do things by myself because I'm a bit controlling, and I feel that if I don't do something it might not get done. Here is an example of what I mean: One day, my son, Olek, was preparing for his son's bris and I said to him, "Listen, you don't have to do everything yourself. You are busy with work. Give me a job to do. Give Dad a job, too. Let us do something." He said to me, "Mom, one time a wise lady taught me that if I don't do things myself, they won't get done." What goes around certainly comes around!

It could be that my marriage has spanned so many years in part because Markus and I are so different in that respect. Once we decide to do something, we make it a goal. But Markus takes his time. He's not like me in that way. I try to get things done right away. Olek is like me and follows in my footsteps. Felicia is like her father.

Make wise choices in life. This is very important. Always be willing to try everything – even including new types of food. Don't say you don't like something without trying it. You must try it. Or don't say you don't like this profession or that profession. If you don't try something, you will never know if it might have been right for you. Try as many different things as you can. Date different types of people. All of this will help you to make wise choices. I began making wise choices for myself at the age of seven when I decided I wanted to become a doctor.

The story becomes a bit hazy when it comes to the choice of a life partner. After all, such a choice is not much like choosing what to cook for dinner. Some choices are more complicated than others. At age 17, my match was arranged by my grandmother. At first, that was all I knew about it. As it turned out, she matched me with my first love. Of course, I didn't know anything about relationships then. I have always been monogamous, one guy at a time. I would go out with a guy and see how it went and if it didn't work out then I would start seeing another one. I have always been very loyal. I think I got that from my star sign. I'm a Leo. And then it was quite a few years and one very reluctant and unconventional blind date before my path crossed with my perfect match, Markus. I never could have guessed that I was meeting the man I would marry that night, but I did. I gave it a chance, and I found the one for me.

I also want to implore you to never lose hope. There are bad things in life that can happen, but when they do, with hope those things will get better. Don't compromise your life goals just to have fun. Stick to your plan, finish college, and the fun will come after that. To prove that last point, two years ago I had a frank discussion with my step-grandson, Yair, Markus' son's son. He was visiting us in Florida from Israel, where young people are required to serve three years in the army. Usually, after the army, most go back to college. But after the army, Yair had taken a year off and then another year off just to have fun. I sat down and had a drink with him, and I said, "Let's talk." He was going return to Israel a few days later. We talked about love and about girlfriends. We spoke in general but the main thing I think he learned from me was that I was very firm on the idea that you cannot become a millionaire if you don't go to college. I told him, "First, learn your work. After that, a lot of good things will happen for you. Having fun will come later in life." I think he did learn from me because after that talk he stuck with his studies. I said to Markus, "Look. He's studying." And Markus said to me, "It's you, honey. You did it again."

The story does not end there. Yair and I continued our discussion.

I told him that in four years after he had completed his studies, we would pay for his ticket to Florida for another visit. I said that I didn't want to hear from him before that, that he wasn't welcome here until he had completed college. That he just had to sit and study. That would be his job. Yair was in his early twenties at the time, and he took my advice and is working on his degree. That airline ticket is still waiting for him when he's ready for it and I'm sure he will achieve it.

As a pioneer for women in dentistry, I hope that my energy, and gentle touch paved the way for other women. My focus on helping women succeed never stopped, although I feel there remains work to be done and goals to reach. The only thing that we have not seen yet in America is a woman president and I hope it happens during my lifetime. There are many more women now involved in politics than there were in the past, which is very good. And there will be more again in the future. Women are so hardworking, and yet they must constantly prove themselves, just like how I worked hard to prove that I was as good or even better than the next guy.

I have no desire, like some people do, to be someone else or live someone else's life. That's not my way. I want to be who I am. I don't want to change. Anyway, I don't think anybody could change me.

Meanwhile, in heaven, I know Grandma Anetta is smiling.

ABOUT THE AUTHOR

Dr. Anna Kohen. Photo credit: Bashkim Hasani

Dr. Anna Kohen, DDS, was born in Vlora, Albania, just after the end of World War II and grew up in a small community of Romaniote Jews that Muslim Albanians had saved from the Nazis. Her family then experienced the hardships of the communist dictatorship. Managing to leave Albania with her family in 1966 through careful planning and trickery, she first settled in Greece, where she completed her dentistry studies at the Ethnikon and Kapodistriakon University of Athens Dental School. Emigrating to the United States in 1971, she continued her studies at New York University's Dental School and received a DDS Dental Degree in 1976. After graduation she was appointed as an Assistant Clinical Professor of Restorative Dentistry at NYU Dental School and taught there for ten years. She practiced general dentistry at her office in Manhattan until her retirement to Sarasota, Florida in 2013.

In 1990, with the help of several Jewish organizations, Dr. Kohen brought 37 of her Jewish-Albanian relatives to the US, and assisted them in the process of integration. In 1991, she was invited to Albania to celebrate the formation of the Albanian Israeli Society, of which she is an elected an Honorary Member. In 2004, the President of the Albanian Republic, Alfred Moisiu, recognized Dr. Kohen with the *Special Civil Merits* medal for, "Valuable contributions helping Albanians during the Kosovar humanitarian crisis; for precious aid given to the new Albanian emigrants in the United States of America." In 2006, Dr. Kohen was given the title Honored Citizen of Vlora by the Major of Vlora. On that same day, Dr. Kohen witnessed the renaming of a street where her Jewish community had lived to "The Jewish Street," the results of her efforts to have Albania's Jewish community recognized. In 2013, the New York Chapter of American Albanian National Organization gave her its Lifetime Achievement Award. Another Albanian President, Bujar Nishani, honored Dr. Kohen during his official visit to Washington, DC, in 2014.

Dr. Kohen's nonprofit work includes assisting the Fresh Air Fund in sending numerous underprivileged children to summer camp, aiding Allen Healthcare provide free classes Albanian immigrants to become home attendants for Albanian elderly, and in partnership with the Italian Cancer Society, helping provide free mammograms to Albanian women without insurance at the Bronx House. She has assisted the Domenick Scaglione Children's Foundation in Tirana, the Little Baby Face Foundation, and partnered with Gift Of Life International to provide Albanian children with lifesaving heart surgeries.

Dr. Kohen frequently visits Albanian schools in the Bronx, teaching children how to take care of their teeth and maintain good oral hygiene. She has participated in countless community events and contributed moral, emotional and financial support to members of the Albanian community. For nearly two decades, she was elected and served as President of the Albanian American Women's Organization — "Motrat Qiriazi" — the most active organization in the Albanian community. She founded and is president of AAWO's Florida chapter. In 2016, Dr. Kohen accepted a Golden Eagle Award at the Diaspora Summit in Albania on behalf of AAWO. In 2018, she was presented with the Lifetime Achievement Award from AAWO in

New York on International Women's Day and Teachers' Day. In 2019, she was honored by the Jewish Federation of Sarasota-Manatee, where she is the founding chair of its International Holocaust Remembrance Day. She has spoken before the United Nations, is an Honorary Member of the Albanian Medical Society, and was honored with a Proclamation from New York City Hall. Dr. Kohen is married to a Holocaust survivor from Poland and has two children and three grandchildren.

ACKNOWLEDGMENTS

I'd like to thank Curt Werner, who took my memories and stories and helped me write them down in this book. My editor, Tony D'Souza, who helped give the book clarity, order, and flow. He checked all the research with patience and moved us along to publication with a positive attitude. Thank you to Viktor Koen, Chair – Illustration Department, School of Visual Arts, for creating the amazing book cover. Many thanks to all the people who wrote advance praise for *Flower of Vlora*, including Zanet Battinou, Michlean Lowry Amir, Agron Alibali, Felicita Jakoel, Dr. Petrit Zorba, Barbara Gilford, and Dr. Shaban Sinani. You are all such highly accomplished and respected people, and I am so grateful for your support. Thank you so very much to Saimir A. Lolja for writing the wonderful introduction, which clearly explains how the Albanian concept of "Besa" led to the salvation of the Jews in Albania.

I am thankful to my friend Sheila Wolf for her encouragement to write the book and reminding me of the importance of sharing my stories with my grandchildren. Thank you to the AAWO Board, who got so excited about the book, they are ready to have a book-signing tour for me! Thank you to my dearest niece, Dr. Ninette Cohen, for believing in me and supporting my charity work. Thank you to Zhana Bozo for helping me remember your parents' Holocaust story. Thank you to my brother, Abe, for filling in the gaps of some of our family stories. Many thanks to Gail Shirazi for her countless recommendations. Thank you to Dr. Mimis Cohen for all his helpful suggestions. To Shqipe Malushi, thank you for your help with the AAWO chapter and staying true to the history.

Last but not least, thank you to everyone at Amsterdam

Publishers, especially Liesbeth Heenk, for believing in *Flower of Vlora* enough to bring it into print.

As Jesse Owens said, "We all have dreams. But in order to make dreams come into reality, it takes an awful lot of determination, dedication, self-discipline, and effort."

PHOTOS

A Romaniote-Jewish couple in traditional clothing in Greece before WWII.

*A young Romaniote-Jewish woman, Simha Koen, in Ioannina,
Greece. The vibrant Romaniote community of Ioannina perished in
Nazi death camps.*

Anna's maternal grandparents, Avraam and Stamula Hatzi, center, with Anna's uncle Nessim top left, her mother Nina, and uncle Isaak top right, in Ioannina, Greece around 1935. Only Nina and Isaak survived WWII.

Anna's father, David Kohen, in Greece around 1935 before the family moved to Albania, where they would survive WWII, unlike most Greek Jews.

The Main Mosque, Vlora Albania. Albanian Muslims saved Anna's family from the Nazis.

*Kadri Lazaj and his wife Vera, the Muslim Albanian saviors of
Anna's family.*

A rare photo of the Kadri Lazaj family in Trevllazër, Albania in 1944.

Top row left to right, Anna's aunt Zhuli Kohen, her father David and mother Nina. Middle row, her grandfather Elia and grandmother Anetta. Bottom row, her older brother Elio, younger brother Abe, and Anna.

Isak Koen and his family in Vlora in 1939. Isak was the acting Romaniote rabbi in Vlora, and all Jewish holidays were celebrated at his home in secret.

Anna, right, with her Muslim friend and classmate Cela in Vlora around 1955.

The only existing photo of the whole family. Top from left, Anna's brotTher Elio, grandfather Elia, mother Nina, father David. Bottom from left, Anna's sister Alice, grandmother Anetta, brother Abe, and Anna in Vlora in the late 1950s.

The family rinsing dyed scarves in the saltwater at the beach as part of the work of the family business, around 1960.

Anna and her older brother Elio, top, with her friend Eli and sister Alice at the beach in Vlora.

Anna and her sister Alice at the beach in Vlora in the early 1960s.

Anna in the hat, around 16 years old, at the beach house in Vlora in the early 1960s.

Anna's high school friends in Vlora in the early 1960s.

Anna, center, in medical school in Tirana in 1964.

Anna on her 'blind' first date with Markus at the Zappion Pavilion in Astoria, New York City.

Anna's grandmother Anetta, seated, at her sister Alice's wedding in 1972 in New York City. From top left, Elio, his wife Telenia, Anna's father David, mother Nina, Alice, her groom Joseph Masri, Anna and Abe.

Anna and Markus's wedding, March 1975.

Anna teaching at the NYU dental school, where she taught from 1976 - 1986.

Anna at the University of Tirana Dental School with the Albanian professors she taught cosmetic dentistry to on her first visit back to Albania in 1989. Behind them is a portrait of the dictator, Enver Hoxha.

Anna with Dr. Zino Matathia and his wife, Valentina, at the Hotel Dajti in Tirana, 1989. Anna and Zino grew up together in Vlora.

Anna, center left, with opera singer Inva Mula and Albanian professors after Anna's lecture at the University of Tirana, 1989.

Anna with her father, David, welcoming Aunt Zhuli and the 37 Albanian Jews immigrants at JFK airport in 1991.

Anna with her father, David, welcoming Aunt Zhuli the 37 Albanian Jews immigrants at JFK airport in 1991.

Anna's mother Nina and uncle Isaak, the only WWII survivors of seven siblings, in Israel in the early 1990s.

Anna and her husband Markus with Refik Veseli, the first Albanian honored by Yad Vashem as Righteous Among the Nations for saving Jews during WWII. 1995.

The President of Albania, Alfred Moisiu, presenting Anna in 2004 with a medal for Special Merit for her humanitarian efforts helping refugees during the Kosovo War.

The plaque for the Jewish Street in Vlora, a cultural heritage and a dedication from Anna Kohen.

The street in Vlora where Anna grew up and that was the heart of the Jewish community was renamed 'The Jewish Street' with this plaque unveiled in a 2006 ceremony. The renaming and plaque were Anna's ideas, the result of her efforts and vision.

*Anna and Markus with Roko Lazaj and his family in Trevllazër,
Albania, in 2012. Roko is the only surviving child of the family who
hid Anna's family during WWII*

*Anna in Trevllazër, Albania, in front of the house where her family
hid from the Nazis during WWII.*

Anna holding the Golden Eagle award during the 2016 Diaspora Summit in Tirana. From left, Albanian Ambassador to the UN, Besiana Kadare, Beti Beno, Anna, the Kosovo Ambassador to the UN, Teuta Sahatqija, and Esmeralda Mosko.

Anna represented Albania at the first celebration of Albanian Independence at New York's City Hall in 2019

Anna's brother Elio's daughter Malkita with her family at their home in Thessaloniki, Greece.

Anna's late brother Elio's daughter Ninette Koen and her family. From left, Ninette's husband Viktor Koen, daughter Sivan, Anna, Ninette's son Elio, Markus and Ninette in New York City, 2018.

*Anna, Markus, Markus's granddaughter Yasmin, Yasmin's father
and Markus's son Alan, and Anna and Markus's son Olek.*

*Anna and Markus with their daughter, Felicia, granddaughter,
Alana, and Chris, in Sarasota in 2021.*

Anna and Markus in Sarasota, Florida, March 2022.

AMSTERDAM PUBLISHERS HOLOCAUST LIBRARY

The series **Holocaust Survivor Memoirs World War II** consists of the following autobiographies of survivors:

Outcry. Holocaust Memoirs, by Manny Steinberg

Hank Brodt Holocaust Memoirs. A Candle and a Promise, by Deborah Donnelly

The Dead Years. Holocaust Memoirs, by Joseph Schupack

Rescued from the Ashes. The Diary of Leokadia Schmidt, Survivor of the Warsaw Ghetto, by Leokadia Schmidt

My Lvov. Holocaust Memoir of a twelve-year-old Girl, by Janina Hescheles

Remembering Ravensbrück. From Holocaust to Healing, by Natalie Hess

Wolf. A Story of Hate, by Zeev Scheinwald with Ella Scheinwald

Save my Children. An Astonishing Tale of Survival and its Unlikely Hero, by Leon Kleiner with Edwin Stepp

Holocaust Memoirs of a Bergen-Belsen Survivor & Classmate of Anne Frank, by Nanette Blitz Konig

Defiant German - Defiant Jew. A Holocaust Memoir from inside the Third Reich, by Walter Leopold with Les Leopold

In a Land of Forest and Darkness. The Holocaust Story of two Jewish Partisans, by Sara Lustigman Omelinski

Holocaust Memories. Annihilation and Survival in Slovakia, by Paul Davidovits

From Auschwitz with Love. The Inspiring Memoir of Two Sisters' Survival, Devotion and Triumph Told by Manci Grunberger Beran & Ruth Grunberger Mermelstein, by Daniel Seymour

Remetz. Resistance Fighter and Survivor of the Warsaw Ghetto, by Jan Yohay Remetz

My March Through Hell. A Young Girl's Terrifying Journey to Survival, by Halina Kleiner with Edwin Stepp

---

The series **Holocaust Survivor True Stories WWII** consists of the following biographies:

Among the Reeds. The true story of how a family survived the Holocaust, by Tammy Bottner

A Holocaust Memoir of Love & Resilience. Mama's Survival from Lithuania to America, by Ettie Zilber

Living among the Dead. My Grandmother's Holocaust Survival Story of Love and Strength, by Adena Bernstein Astrowsky

Heart Songs. A Holocaust Memoir, by Barbara Gilford

Shoes of the Shoah. The Tomorrow of Yesterday, by Dorothy Pierce

Hidden in Berlin. A Holocaust Memoir, by Evelyn Joseph Grossman

Separated Together. The Incredible True WWII Story of Soulmates Stranded an Ocean Apart, by Kenneth P. Price, Ph.D.

The Man Across the River. The incredible story of one man's will to survive the Holocaust, by Zvi Wiesenfeld

If Anyone Calls, Tell Them I Died. A Memoir, by Emanuel (Manu) Rosen

The House on Thrömerstrasse. A Story of Rebirth and Renewal in the Wake of the Holocaust, by Ron Vincent

Dancing with my Father. His hidden past. Her quest for truth. How Nazi Vienna shaped a family's identity, by Jo Sorochinsky

The Story Keeper. Weaving the Threads of Time and Memory - A Memoir, by Fred Feldman

Krisia's Silence. The Girl who was not on Schindler's List, by Ronny Hein

Defying Death on the Danube. A Holocaust Survival Story, by Debbie J. Callahan with Henry Stern

A Doorway to Heroism. A decorated German-Jewish Soldier who became an American Hero, by Rabbi W. Jack Romberg

The Shoemaker's Son. The Life of a Holocaust Resister, by Laura Beth Bakst

The Redhead of Auschwitz. A True Story, by Nechama Birnbaum

Land of Many Bridges. My Father's Story, by Bela Ruth Samuel Tenenholtz

Creating Beauty from the Abyss. The Amazing Story of Sam Herciger, Auschwitz Survivor and Artist, by Lesley Ann Richardson

On Sunny Days We Sang. A Holocaust Story of Survival and Resilience, by Jeannette Grunhaus de Gelman

Painful Joy. A Holocaust Family Memoir, by Max J. Friedman

I Give You My Heart. A True Story of Courage and Survival, by Wendy Holden

In the Time of Madmen, by Mark A. Prelas

Monsters and Miracles. Horror, Heroes and the Holocaust, by Ira Wesley Kitmacher

Flower of Vlora. Growing up Jewish in Communist Albania, by Anna Kohen

Aftermath: Coming of Age on Three Continents. A Memoir, by Annette Libeskind Berkovits

Not a real Enemy. The True Story of a Hungarian Jewish Man's Fight for Freedom, by Robert Wolf

Zaidy's War. Four Armies, Three Continents, Two Brothers. One Man's Impossible Story of Endurance, by Martin Bodek

The Glassmaker's Son. Looking for the World my Father left behind in Nazi Germany, by Peter Kupfer

The Apprentice of Buchenwald. The True Story of the Teenage Boy Who Sabotaged Hitler's War Machine, by Oren Schneider

The Cello Still Sings. A Generational Story of the Holocaust and of the Transformative Power of Music, by Janet Horvath

––––––

The series **Jewish Children in the Holocaust** consists of the following autobiographies of Jewish children hidden during WWII in the Netherlands:

Searching for Home. The Impact of WWII on a Hidden Child, by Joseph Gosler

See You Tonight and Promise to be a Good Boy! War memories, by Salo Muller

Sounds from Silence. Reflections of a Child Holocaust Survivor, Psychiatrist and Teacher, by Robert Krell

Sabine's Odyssey. A Hidden Child and her Dutch Rescuers, by Agnes Schipper

The Journey of a Hidden Child, by Harry Pila with Robin Black

---

The series **New Jewish Fiction** consists of the following novels, written by Jewish authors. All novels are set in the time during or after the Holocaust.

The Corset Maker. A Novel, by Annette Libeskind Berkovits

Escaping the Whale. The Holocaust is over. But is it ever over for the next generation? by Ruth Rotkowitz

When the Music Stopped. Willy Rosen's Holocaust, by Casey Hayes

Hands of Gold. One Man's Quest to Find the Silver Lining in Misfortune, by Roni Robbins

The Girl Who Counted Numbers. A Novel, by Roslyn Bernstein

There was a garden in Nuremberg. A Novel, by Navina Michal Clemerson

The Butterfly and the Axe, by Omer Bartov

Good for a Single Journey, by Helen Joyce

The series **Holocaust Books for Young Adults** consists of the following novels, based on true stories:

The Boy behind the Door. How Salomon Kool Escaped the Nazis. Inspired by a True Story, by David Tabatsky

Running for Shelter. A True Story, by Suzette Sheft

The Precious Few. An Inspirational Saga of Courage based on True Stories, by David Twain with Art Twain

Jacob's Courage: A Holocaust Love Story, by Charles S. Weinblatt

———

The series **WW2 Historical Fiction** consists of the following novels, some of which are based on true stories:

Mendelevski's Box. A Heartwarming and Heartbreaking Jewish Survivor's Story, by Roger Swindells

A Quiet Genocide. The Untold Holocaust of Disabled Children WW2 Germany, by Glenn Bryant

The Knife-Edge Path, by Patrick T. Leahy

Brave Face. The Inspiring WWII Memoir of a Dutch/German Child, by I. Caroline Crocker and Meta A. Evenly

When We Had Wings. The Gripping Story of an Orphan in Janusz Korczak's Orphanage. A Historical Novel, by Tami Shem-Tov

Want to be an AP book reviewer?

Reviews are very important in a world dominated by the social media and social proof. Please drop us a line if you want to join the *AP review team*. We will then add you to our list of advance reviewers. No strings attached, and we promise that we will not be spamming you.

info@amsterdampublishers.com

42148725R00139